Praise for

Brand Aid

"Everyone has a personal brand, the key to success and failure is how we manage it. This book provides a great practical guide to achieve your best personal brand today."
—Erik Qualman, bestselling author of *Socialnomics* and *Digital Leader*

"A must-read guide to understanding the most important issue of our digitally connected world—your personal brand."
—Mitch Thrower, cofounder of Active.com and founder of BUMP.com and Events.com

"This well-written, straightforward, and informative book demystifies the dark arts of branding and lays them bare for the everyman without the brand witch-doctor mumbo-jumbo. It strikes the perfect balance between practical advice and knowledge that will allow you to adapt and evolve your brand for the rest of your life."
—Steve Farnsworth, executive director of Silicon Valley Brand Forum

"A deep dive into a complex topic which offers real-world advice. A powerful must-read for anyone anywhere."
—Alexander Boylan, executive producer of Around the World Productions, and winner of *The Amazing Race 2*

"Whether you are a college freshman or CEO of a Fortune 500, this book is the only resource you'll need in order to identify, develop, and proactively manage a powerful personal brand."
—Roger Looyenga, former CEO and chairman of the board of Auto-Owners Insurance and author of *Take the Stairs*

"This is a book that needs to be read by anybody in business that wants to make a difference. If you think personal branding is the social media equivalent of bragging, get over it." —Mike Natalizio, CEO of HNI

BRAND AID

Taking Control of Your Reputation—
Before Everyone Else Does

Larry G. Linne
and
Patrick Sitkins

PRENTICE HALL PRESS

PRENTICE HALL PRESS
Published by the Penguin Group
Penguin Group (USA) LLC
375 Hudson Street, New York, New York 10014

USA • Canada • UK • Ireland • Australia • New Zealand • India • South Africa • China

penguin.com

A Penguin Random House Company

Prentice Hall Press trade paperback ISBN: 978-0-7352-0541-3

The Library of Congress has cataloged the Prentice Hall Press hardcover edition as follows:

Linne, Larry G.
Brand aid : taking control of your reputation—before everyone else does /
Larry G. Linne and Patrick Sitkins.—First edition.
pages cm
ISBN 978-0-7352-0536-9
1. Reputation.   2. Character.   3. Public opinion.   4. Branding (Marketing)
I. Sitkins, Patrick.   II. Title.
BJ1531.L56 2014
650.1'3—dc23   2013035032

PUBLISHING HISTORY
Prentice Hall Press trade paperback edition / January 2015
Prentice Hall Press hardcover edition / January 2014
Originally published as *Brand Damage* by AuthorHouse in 2013.

PRINTED IN THE UNITED STATES OF AMERICA

10   9   8   7   6   5   4   3   2   1

Text design by Laura K. Corless

Most Prentice Hall Press books are available at special quantity discounts for bulk purchases for
sales promotions, premiums, fund-raising, or educational use. Special books, or book excerpts, can
also be created to fit specific needs. For details, write: Special.Markets@us.penguingroup.com.

CONTENTS

FOREWORD

Long before the Internet, when the world was just a series of villages and larger towns, before the technologies and advancements that made interconnectivity possible were ever conceived, your reputation was based on what you did and how the people around you perceived your actions.

Without highways, transportation, cell phones, and meaningful communications mechanisms that consistently linked one town to another, your reputation was confined to a small geographic area and a relatively constrained number of people.

That meant a fresh start was nearly always possible for those with the daring, means, and wherewithal to strike out for a new destination.

Flash forward to right now.

We are all residents of the Internet, the world's largest community—where everyone could very well learn your name, age, political affiliations, religious beliefs, and other salient personal details—all courtesy of the dawn of the Digital Age.

Without any announcement or fanfare, the Internet has changed what it means to have a reputation.

A new beginning, a reinvention of self, is not possible in this era in the same way it was before. The Internet (almost) never forgets. Make a mistake—no matter how young you were and how exemplary you've been since—and you're in the digital stocks of the

Internet's town square forever, on the receiving end of judgment from next-door neighbors to strangers thousands of miles away. Mistaken for someone else? The Internet doesn't care. You could wear the virtual equivalent of a Scarlet Letter in perpetuity.

The Internet, for good or for ill, has totally and irrevocably changed the landscape of interaction and interconnection without announcing it. There's no going back. It's a one-way ratchet, where your digital reputation will get more important over time, not less important. It's a dynamic, shifting world and like it or not, it's one you must get smart about—and quickly.

The Internet is most people's first preferred source when it comes to information, a Pew Research Center study demonstrated. What's more, other research shows that almost 90 percent of people never go beyond a basic "sniff test" when looking for information about you, and they *rely* on the meager data they find first when making decisions about you.

Here's what that research says to me: people are looking for you and, for better or worse, what they find is your new digital résumé. It's your personal brand.

So have you Googled yourself lately?

That's what the people in your life—or who are presently on its periphery—are doing. Whether it's the girl at the coffee shop who got your number, a prospective client, a hiring manager finishing her due diligence, candidates for employment, the PTA president at your child's school, or a landlord verifying your details—the possibilities are endless and the ramifications are simply too important, too crucial, to take lightly. They have a real, meaningful, and measurable impact on your life—whether it's personally, professionally, romantically, or economically.

And what happens if they find the kind of information that the

Internet is so good at serving up: incomplete or obsolete data, or half truth, innuendo, suggestion, or falsehood? Or what happens when they find information about someone who shares your name and think that they're finding information about you? What happens then?

Well, then comes the thundering silence.

The sound of your phone *not* ringing is almost the worst thing to hear. Everybody is looking you up online, and everybody is relying on what they find. And when they see something that makes them suspicious, they don't bother telling you they've found something worrisome. They just don't call you back. They assume that smoke equals fire, and they go looking for another candidate, another vendor, another date, or another provider.

And what if you're one of the few people with almost no information online? You may be congratulating yourself that you "don't post pictures or anything," so you should be okay. Right? You may think that you're in the clear. No news is good news, after all.

Wrong.

If there's a big absence of information when people search for you online, that's also bad. The Internet has conditioned us to expect to find some amount of data on everyone so when we can't find anything, it raises our eyebrows. It can even make us suspicious. We might not be able to pinpoint exactly what the issue is—just that it seems vaguely wrong.

But most important for you, it is a huge—as in, *mega*!—missed opportunity to establish your personal brand. To help people understand who you really are. To define yourself—before the vagaries of a search engine algorithm or another person do it for you.

The same principle holds true when there's a mismatch in what someone values in real life and what's reflected about her online.

Take, for example, a person who claims to be a passionate, committed environmental engineer. She's applying for a job at a nonprofit conservation organization. But everything found about her online reflects her other passion for Harry Potter stories. Nothing about the environmental engineering that the person claimed was her passion, her life. She will lose that opportunity she so strongly desires.

This is the era of the Pull Economy. We can also call it the Reputation Economy. In the past, we used to *apply* for everything in the Push Economy. We'd apply for jobs by sending (pushing) our résumés. We'd "apply" for new customers by marketing (pushing) our services in the media.

Now the market reaches out to us. If you develop a personal brand as an expert in environmental engineering—a brand that will exist almost entirely online—employers will find you. By developing a personal brand as a key consultant, you will "pull" customers to you.

That's the Pull Economy. Of course, we still advertise, market, and "push." But increasingly, both our lead-generation marketing and our conversion marketing happen at the moment of "pull."

And whether the market pulls your way or not—yep, you guessed it—depends on your reputation.

The Internet is our everyday, global arena, where our lives (at least portions of them) play out in high-stakes exhibitions. It's the public theater where audiences we've never personally seen or met can catch glimpses of us—from our working lives to our personal narratives—and come away thinking they know who we are.

The good news is that we *can* do something about this, which is precisely why I started my company, Reputation.com. We develop patented technologies to manage personal and corporate reputations as well as protect your digital privacy. When the Internet wrongs you, there is no court of appeals. Where do you turn in the imper-sonal space of bits and bytes, 1s and 0s, to find relief?

The answer is empowerment.

Sometimes that's turning to technology solutions and expert counsel like ours.

Sometimes it starts with you.

There are always things that you can do personally—that don't cost much in the way of money but do require methodical thought, care, and effort—to start the process of building your personal brand and take back control of how you're represented, online and offline.

That's why you'll find the practical advice in *Brand Aid* to be so powerful. Larry Linne and Patrick Sitkins outline memorable examples—from corporations to their own personal lives—that can help you see just how valuable building, curating, and caring for your personal brand will be to you. In addition to learning what you *ought* to do, they'll illuminate the "Steer Clears" for you—the com-mon pitfalls and problems of personal branding that can derail even your best efforts to make a difference for yourself.

You'll begin to see that with both offensive and defensive strate-gies, you can get leaps and bounds closer to bulletproofing that brand. There's a reason why that old adage, "An ounce of prevention is worth a pound of cure," is called so easily to mind: it's true. I have years of practical experience working with Fortune 500 companies, celebrities, and government leaders on this very issue. There is no doubt that the more effort you sink into building your personal brand now, the greater the dividends pay out later, typically right at the time they'll be most helpful to you.

The bottom line is that the issue of reputation management in the Digital Age is a growing problem—not a shrinking one.

No matter where you are in life or where you're going, you'll need to thoughtfully consider what your personal brand should be, how it could and should evolve over time, and the steps you can take to build a credible brand.

In the pages that follow, Larry and Patrick will show you how.

—Michael Fertik
CEO and founder of Reputation.com
Author of *The Wild West 2.0* and
The Reputation Economy (forthcoming)

It takes many good deeds to build a good reputation, and only one bad one to lose it.

—Benjamin Franklin

INTRODUCTION

In 2002, I spoke to a group of Canadian and U.S. business executives about the power and importance of personal branding. You would have thought I was communicating blasphemy. The feedback was harsh. It was considered "selfish" to brand yourself. They saw personal branding as something you would do as an actor, athlete, or someone who was trying to draw attention to him or herself. In a world where teams were the focus of business, it just seemed out of place to accept and promote personal branding.

My speech was not well received and was dismissed as a needed business strategy. Undeterred, I have continued to manage my personal brand through the past twelve years, and have helped individuals who buy into the process. Still, many continued to reject the concept. It wasn't until 2010 that I finally was able to clearly articulate a compelling reason why someone should manage his or her brand.

The trends in the past ten years have naturally swayed toward greater acceptance, for many of the reasons outlined in this book. The most compelling reason, however, came from the definition we are using for "brand." A brand is what people think of you. So, when I speak today to business leaders, I ask them to write down what others think of them. I ask them to identify what personal attributes they would most benefit from if those items were well-known to those with whom they interact personally and professionally. Then I reveal to them the truth. If they wrote down anything when asked what others think of them, they have a brand. If they wrote down anything when asked if they had attributes to highlight, they have a "desired brand."

> A brand is what people think of you.

In a recent workshop with a group of fifty salespeople, I had them do this branding exercise. Each of them wrote down what they believed people thought of them. I asked them to include what friends, family, coworkers, and acquaintances may say about them. I encouraged them to write down all positive, negative, and neutral things that they believed others would say in an anonymous request to describe what they think of them. After they had written down a list of items, I asked them to write down what they would want people to think of them, if they wanted to get the most out of those relationships. The fifty salespeople were all shocked at how different the first list was from the second. They realized they had allowed others to perceive or focus on certain things about them that were not the most beneficial in their relationships.

Next we discussed how they could slightly alter behaviors and be more purposeful. The point of this discussion was to show them how minor adjustments in their behavior could make the second list (desired brand) a reality. They could do little things like participate more proactively in conversations, make purposeful choice of dress and appearance on different occasions, and other simple behavior changes. (We will address many of these ideas in the following chapters.)

Many people will say that they feel "misunderstood." Well, I believe it is because they have sent a brand message that is different from the real them. Too often, branding is thought of as something only corporations do, or something that would be too arduous or impractical for an individual to undertake. In the busy-ness of modern life, it gets lost on a theoretical to-do list and never gets addressed with a concrete plan. Of course, this means your brand is defined by default, left to the whims of chance and the perceptions of others. To call this a missed opportunity is an understatement. Instead, I would call it a recipe for being misunderstood. (In Chapter 2, we'll cover some basic strategies for anticipating and avoiding being misunderstood.)

The buy-in at my speeches and training becomes much stronger when these realities are introduced. When we show people how often they are being researched on the Internet (as individuals) and therefore how accessible their brand is, they get really interested in personal brand management. It is my belief that personal brand management is going to be a strategic initiative in all businesses by 2015—if they are to survive.

I have thirty years' experience in marketing and branding. I have rebranded hundreds of companies and individuals all over North America, Central America, and Latin America. I have applied the principles you will read about in this book to my companies and products (e.g., Sitkins International, Intellectual Innovations, Make the Noise Go Away, Noise Reduction System, MyExit Strategies, and more). The results of these companies and products have all been greater than expected because of our ability to manage the brand.

I felt the need, however, to bring a younger brand expert into this project as well. I worked with Patrick Sitkins for six years at Sitkins Group Inc. (under the brand Sitkins International). We continued to collaborate when he moved on to his own marketing and branding company, which is now Quintain Marketing. I was honored to mentor Patrick for six years of his career. His skills and understanding around branding have evolved from what I was able to teach him. Patrick is typical of an early thirtysomething marketing guy. He is irreverent, smart, fearless in business, and lives to make a difference. We have worked on many branding projects, and the "iron sharpens iron" concept has worked well in our relationship. Throughout this book, you will hear Patrick's perspective in addition to my own. The combination of my decades of experience in all aspects of branding and Patrick's understanding of modern brand management and technology will provide you with the insights and skills needed to create and manage your personal brand in order to help you achieve success, however you define it. (Both of our ideas appear throughout the book, but when you see the first person used, it's Larry's voice you're reading.)

The subject of personal branding is timelier than ever. The market is now placing much more stock in individuals than in big corporate brands. In the last few years, we have seen powerful, well-known titans of industry fall. Scandals, bailouts, downsizing, massive layoffs, ethical misconduct, and golden parachutes have dominated the headlines. Consumers have taken notice of all of this. Now, more than ever before, the public has become disenfranchised. Millennials and Gen Xers in particular have lost faith in corporate structures and messages. They now rely on word of mouth, social groups, recommendations, and strong connections. The individual is now more important than the organization. What people think about you is now more important than where you work, what school you went to, your social group, or any other entity you're affiliated with. Your brand is what matters most.

> The individual is now more important than the organization.

The principles in this book will not only help you see value in personal branding, but more important, it will give you strategies to consider and will connect you to resources to help you manage your personal brand with a purposeful plan. The information will help you sort through what many see as an overwhelming task with simple steps to help define, maintain, and promote your brand.

Because if you don't, everyone else will.

CHAPTER 1

What's a Brand, and Who Says I Have One?

The way to gain a good reputation is to endeavor to be what you desire to appear.

—Socrates

Personal Branding Starts at Home

Most parents tell their kids they have to manage their reputations. Unfortunately, the word *reputation* has lost its impact. Kids usually translate that into "You don't want me to embarrass our family." Unfortunately for most families, kids are too focused on themselves to be motivated by what others may think of the family. Enter social media. Now our kids' "reputation" is being communicated across the Internet. "What people may think" about our kids is now available at the speed of megahertz.

I have five school-age daughters. Every August, I sit with each of them and ask, "At the end of this school year, what do you want your friends, classmates, and teachers to think about you?" They tell me things like "I was nice, hardworking, inclusive of others, helpful, friendly, good at sports," and more. Each of my girls is unique and has different items on her list. Then I ask them what they must do to guarantee people feel this way about them. They tell me things like "I have to work hard, think about others first, introduce myself to new people, be prepared," and so on. Then I ask them what they have to *not* do or avoid to ensure people think these things about them. They say "Not talk bad about others," "Not post negative things on Facebook," "Not turn in homework late," and so on.

We frequently talk about personal branding and use the definition "what people think about you" in our home. Throughout the year, we have discussions about how they are managing their "brands." We talk about "thinking about your brand" before posting on social media sites. We do self-checks on how we are all doing on personal brand management. It has become a fun activity for us, part of family culture, and our kids have really connected with the concept. I think they see brand management as a cool thing to do. It is very rewarding to hear them teaching their friends about managing their brand.

Okay, time to brag a little. My thirteen-year-old daughter had two examples during the year where she chose to not do things with kids (go to an inappropriate movie and lie about where she was going) because it would "hurt my brand." She uses the term *brand management* as a part of her normal conversation. I heard her tell one friend, "I have a bigger future and can't afford to damage my brand by doing something stupid."

> "I have a bigger future and can't afford to damage my brand by doing something stupid."

My eleven-year-old daughter had a great brand management experience this past year. Her elementary school has an award for graduating fifth-grade students. The award is determined by all of the students writing an essay on another kid they believe represents the character traits the school promotes. Fortunately for my daughter, the character traits align exactly with the "brand" items she identifies at the first of the year.

The kids turn in these essays, and the teachers review the kids with the most essays written about them. Based on what is written and teacher observation from the year, the teachers vote and choose the top character student.

I asked my daughter a week before the award was announced, "How did you do in managing your brand this year?"

She said, "I think I did a good job."

Her mom and I were so proud when we went to graduation and they announced her name as the winner. This was an award based on what others *thought* about our daughter. She realized that her success was due to determining her brand, determining what she had to do and not do, and frequently thinking about and monitoring her brand throughout the year.

My family has realized how much better our lives are when we manage what we want people to think of us. For those who think this is manipulative or controlling, remember that everyone has a brand. Our random behaviors can send a message to others that is not true about us. Now keep in mind that we can't completely control what others think about us. Others may misinterpret our brand or what we want them to think of us. You have a much better chance of getting others to think certain things about you, however, if you're purposeful rather than leaving it to chance.

> You have a much better chance of getting others to think certain things about you if you're purposeful rather than leaving it to chance.

I also believe in managing a brand that truly represents you. You can't hide a false brand for long. You can, however, ruin a great brand with a random mistake due to a lack of awareness. Brand management offers each of us a way to be mindful of our behavior, our relationships, our communications with others, and the person we are striving to be.

Your Personal Brand Matters More Than Ever

What do the following people—Mark Zuckerberg, LeBron James, Jerry Sandusky, Steve Jobs, Hope Solo, and all of your colleagues, friends, and family members—have in common? Every one of them has a personal brand, and every one of them has, or will have, an impact on what others think about the organizations with which they are affiliated because of that brand.

Each of the names listed above gives you an emotion of some type (if you know who they are). That is what a brand does.

Hope Solo is a name that creates both positive and negative emotions, depending on your beliefs. It is hard, however, to think about the U.S. women's soccer team without thinking about Hope Solo.

In recent times, you almost can't think of Penn State without Jerry Sandusky coming to mind.

Steve Jobs and Apple—certainly a natural fit.

Mark Zuckerberg is a name that can create all types of emotions about his style, character, youth, creativity, and more.

Okay, no big deal. This is normal, right? We have always associated big-name people with the organizations to which they belong. Ah, but has something changed?

A 2011 study of the world's top one thousand companies, commissioned by Ernst & Young, found that 832 of those companies had a minimum of a 20 percent decrease in value during the prior five-year period, due to "reputation." Reputation hits were items like data breach, news about individuals in the company, product failures or recalls, political issues, or legal situations. I can't imagine any other time in history where this level of brand damage could have happened.

Lloyd's of London compiles the results of annual surveys pertaining to risk and risk preparedness. The Lloyd's Index 2011 report also revealed the changing nature of reputation and its impact on business. The CEOs identified reputation as the ninth-highest risk out of forty-one different risks in 2009. The CEOs identified reputation as the third-highest risk in 2011.

Yes, times have changed. Individuals are influencing the brands of companies, which will impact the value of those companies.

Looking up People First

We sent a survey out to more than ten thousand business decision makers and asked them to give us feedback on what preparation they do before meeting with a salesperson.

Seventy-eight percent of decision makers look up salespeople before meeting with them. It is critical to understand this fact. More than three out of four decision makers seek out information about salespeople before they call on them. This means the brand of the salespeople precedes them. This is potentially very damaging or a great opportunity. Prior to the Internet, we had to call friends and business associates to learn about people before meeting them. This took too long, and happened only on occasion. Now it is the norm. I ask salespeople in my numerous training classes each year if they have managed what someone would find if they were to be looked up. The majority of the people cringe and immediately begin cleaning up their online presence and starting to manage their brand. I also find that the majority go look me up online within twenty-four hours. Interesting how that comes back around.

Seventy-six percent look up the company prior to meeting with a salesperson. I found this interesting, as well. Fewer people are looking up the company than looking up the person. This was surprising to us. We believed the company brand was still the primary interest. The data spoke differently, and this new reality suggests people are going to look at both when learning about a potential purchase.

> Fewer people are looking up the company than looking up the person.

Ninety-eight percent of decision makers look up details on the company that the salespeople represent if they are still interested after the initial meeting. My work in sales suggests that this is a behavior of reinforcing what they saw or heard from the salesperson. The buyer is simply verifying and doing more thorough research to see if what was said aligns with what is online.

When the buyers researched people, they used the following sources:

- 84 percent used a Google search.

- 65 percent used LinkedIn.

- 58 percent used Facebook.

- 48 percent used Twitter.

- 54 percent searched for personal web pages.

Social media trends will make this data obsolete relatively fast. We found this important to share, however, because these entities will most likely not go away anytime soon. The impact of each and the order in which people use these resources will change over time, and will vary from person to person. The point is not to worry too much about the order; all of them can have an impact. More social media sites will come into existence and will play a role in your brand management in the future.

One of the most recent social media evolutions is on LinkedIn. The site uses algorithms and pulls data from individual sites to push a person's brand out to the market. Words and phrases in a user's profile are extracted and pushed (sent to another user's page to see) to the person's connections for "endorsements." This change has created a headache for many people trying to manage their brand. If the endorsements come in heavy in areas a person doesn't want to highlight, these characteristics will begin to reflect a brand different from the desired brand. Social media will continue to use strategies that create interaction and connectivity. Proactively managing this information is a critical part of effective personal brand management.

On average, decision makers spend 52 percent of their research time on the person with whom they will do business and 48 percent on the company. This data suggests that, since the information is available, buyers are spending time researching the people with whom they will do business . . . or not. People used to be able to influence what others thought about them by talking or acting in a certain way. Now our reputation is built on the past, present, and future.

Before the twenty-first century began, we were only doing word-of-mouth and phone research on companies we were considering for business needs or personal purchases. When the Internet developed enough volume, we moved to more in-depth company searches and much more thorough learning about the people and companies from which we bought products and services. Both of these methods are still being used on different levels. Younger people, however, are more comfortable with non-interpersonal research. The Millennial generation grew up banking without going to a bank, buying music online, and sending mail electronically. It doesn't matter if word-of-mouth or online research is more effective. The shift is going to continue to move to online research. Like it or not, your brand will precede you in most new relationships.

> Your brand will precede you in most new relationships.

I believe this research also shows that we have shifted the focus away from the company product or brand. Don't get me wrong, we are still looking at the company brand. The majority of time and energy, however, is now being spent on the individual brands of the people in the organization. People want to know about the person as much as the company.

> People want to know about the person as much as the company.

This data represents businesses selling to other businesses. The trend, however, is broader than business-to-business sales strategies. This data shows that it is natural and easy to find out about others and to be able to form opinions of people before we meet them. In a world where relationships have a huge impact on our ability to be successful, managing what people think of us can have a very positive impact on our personal success. I would bet that just about everyone in North America has been "looked up" by a prospective client, employer, friend, date, colleague, or someone else.

In the past few months, I have been to several social events during which someone has come up to me and informed me that he had looked me up on the Internet. This includes people my wife invited over to our home, neighbors, country club members, guys on my cycling team, and even the parents of the kids' soccer team. I even had one parent on a soccer team look me up on her iPad while standing next to me on the sidelines of my eight-year-old's game. She tried to be discreet, but when she typed my name in the search bar, the Google results page lit up with my name (relevant and positive information). It was hard to hide—for either of us!

The personal brand train has left the station. Your brand is public and quickly accessible. Actually, some would say "You can't find me on the Internet." Well, even that is evidence of your brand!

If you throw in social media, the Internet (and the speed with which information travels), and cameras on smartphones and cell phones, all of a sudden a single individual in your company has the ability to damage a company brand in a moment of poor judgment.

The wrong thing said to the wrong person. A poor customer service experience posted on YouTube. An illegal act posted on a video or on Facebook. Damaging or positively impacting a brand is now a full-time job. We will show many examples of positive and negative brand management throughout the rest of this book. You can look at the news on a daily basis and see it playing out. When we can learn of major news about people all over the world within a few hours because of Twitter, we have to accept that our brand can no longer be hidden.

Keep in mind that our new era of personal brand management is also an opportunity.

I recently had a company decide to do business with me because they were able to research my 9.5 Alive foundation. This foundation raises money to support orphans and educate women in undeveloped countries. The CEO liked what she saw and made the decision to do business with me because of my brand, even before she learned anything about my product.

Your company brand is a combination of the company and the

individuals in the company. More often than not, in today's business environment, the strength or weakness of your brand will come from individuals.

The Stakes Are High

Recently I was at a board meeting for a large construction association. A new board member, whom I did not know, was attending the session. He was introduced, and only a few people on the board had any knowledge of or relationship with him. He did a great job in the meeting. He was a great listener and offered the right advice at the right time. He was intelligent, had a quick wit, and was very articulate. We were all impressed and felt like we had a great new member of the team.

After the board meeting we had a planned dinner. We started with drinks and some appetizers in the bar area of the restaurant. This new board member went right to the hard liquor, and his personality immediately changed. He became very talkative and inappropriate. He began sharing inside information about his company and colleagues. His voice became very loud, and he was embarrassing to the group, as others were in the restaurant.

I could see people rolling their eyes at him and distancing themselves from him the rest of the night. He sat on the board for the next three years, and he never had as good of a day as that first board meeting. The group treated him differently from that night forward. The other board members believed he couldn't be trusted. Not one person ever became close with him. Associating with him could be very bad for one's brand. His brand was damaged in one night!

Five years later, I was at a meeting in a different state. The meeting was with a group of prominent executives in the construction industry. One of them asked me if I knew the gentleman I spoke of above. I responded that I did know him. Nine of the people at this meeting started talking about him. Some told stories about him, and others expressed how they had "heard about him." All the stories were about his drinking and improper social behavior.

Can this type of brand damage be repaired? Yes, but not overnight. We'll look at repair strategies in Chapter 6. There is always room for redemption. But a problem avoided is a problem solved, which is why the main focus of this book is on fostering, maintaining, and protecting your personal brand—before there's major repair work to be done.

Telling Others What to Think

As I've mentioned, my kids are often my best teachers. My second-oldest daughter, Wen Jun, has taught me more than I could fit into this book. She is from Inner Mongolia, China, and we were blessed to have her come into our family when she was thirteen years old. She has been vision impaired her entire life. She was born with only one eye and cannot see much better than 20/200 out of that eye. She is an amazing young woman and gets around incredibly well without a cane or mobility devices. She probably should be using these mobility devices 100 percent of the time. She adapts quickly to an environment and can get around as well as any fully sighted person does. She is legally blind, however, and will never be able to see perfectly.

Blind and vision-impaired people want to fit in and be normal, just like everyone else. Using mobility devices can make them stand out, and some, particularly teenagers who long to fit in, will feel embarrassed that these devices make them look different. My daughter feels this way and frequently tries to hide her blindness. It is unfortunate, because the reality is that she is amazing in how she can do so much that others can't do. When you realize she is blind, her talent and skills blow you away.

Until recently, Wen Jun never wanted to use her cane in public. She felt it would "brand" her as blind. Rather, she wants to be recognized for her independence, capability, and other fine traits, which are too numerous to list here. Even our best efforts to control how others see us can have unintended consequences, however. I began to notice that when my daughter was out in public without her cane—in a crowded restaurant, for example—people would look at her with distaste. If she bumped into someone's chair or spilled something, she was seen by others as a clumsy, obnoxious teenager without discipline or concern for others. Of course, nothing could be further from the truth. But the irritated expressions of others revealed how they saw her, and it wasn't pretty.

When she takes her cane with her, the picture is an entirely different one. She might walk into someone by accident or knock something over when walking by a table. People quickly look at her with respect and smile at her. They see that she is dealing with vision impairment and realize they couldn't do what she is doing!

> Even our best efforts to control how others see us can have unintended consequences.

Watching Wen Jun through this struggle has helped me to understand brand management better. I see that *we can influence what others think of us in so many ways.* We can choose to let our brand be defined by default, or we can tell others what to think of us. Just the use of her mobility devices can dramatically change how people perceive her. What we wear, how we carry ourselves, and how we present ourselves are all preemptive messages about our brand.

But Wen Jun and her cane have taught me something else, too.

Her original intention to avoid being perceived as disabled led to her being seen as careless and inconsiderate. Her attempts to shape her brand were misinterpreted (more on this later). In Wen Jun's particular case, she wasn't able to see—literally—how people perceived her. This is where the help of trusted friends and loved ones comes in. When I advised her of the way others were reacting to her behavior, she revised her game plan. This course correction made all the difference. Because while we

> While we can influence how others see us, we can't control their opinion 100 percent.

can influence how others see us, we can't control their opinion 100 percent. With honest feedback from trusted sources, we can maintain our brand without compounding unintended misperceptions.

I cannot imagine the difficulty of what my daughter must go through in facing these challenges every day. I will never be able to completely understand. I am thankful that she has helped me learn more about brand management (and so much more) through her struggles. When I read this section to her, she got very excited. She said, "Dad, I hope others will be able to be better from my experience." Pretty cool kid.

Trusting Your Instincts Isn't Enough

One of my other daughters recently taught me yet another lesson about personal branding. She had just broken up with a very nice kid. She did it gracefully and made sure to try to protect his ego and confidence (as much as you can when breaking up). She immediately opened up her Facebook page on her cell phone and started to change her status to "single." I stopped her and asked, "How will that impact your brand?"

She looked at me and said, "I guess it will probably hurt his feelings and hurt his ego. So I will look like I am rubbing it in his face. I will look mean. It will cause him to post 'single' on his status, and he may say some negative things about me."

I gave her a smile and said, "Okay, and what do you want people to think about when they think of you?"

She smiled back, as we have had this kind of conversation on a regular basis. "I want people to think of me as nice and as someone who treats others with respect."

"So how are you going to manage your brand on Facebook with this breakup?"

"Well, Dad, I think I could let him change his status first. Then I can make a positive statement about him on his post. Then I can change my status. Then people may see me as a nice person, and he may have a hard time saying mean things to me."

I smiled, and she knew she had nailed that one (the look on her face was priceless).

She followed through, and it played out beautifully. The next day he posted that he was single, and she immediately posted what a great guy he is and how much she had enjoyed being in a relationship with him. He immediately responded back and said very positive things about my daughter. He called her classy, smart, and one of the best people he had ever known.

Over the next couple of days, many other people posted on this status change. Adults, friends of both kids, and family members all posted incredibly nice things about both of these kids. By simply asking the question "How will this impact my brand?" she was able to have a very strong brand management experience versus the potential negative one that would have been triggered by her natural instinct.

This may be the primary reason that Patrick and I have found this topic to be so powerful. Our natural instincts are not always the best things to follow when it comes to personal brand management. As a society, and as individuals, we don't have enough experience with social media in a world where information comes at us at an incredibly high speed. In addition, when we act out of emotion, without purpose and focus on the bigger picture of the image we want to protect, we often harm our brand. We react, post, and then see what happens. Most people I know have experiences of doing something stupid on social media. This is the equivalent of standing on the table in a crowded restaurant and ranting at the top of your lungs. You'll make an impact, but it might not be the one you want to have. What's worse, unlike in a crowded restaurant, you won't necessarily see the reaction on others' faces. You might not even be aware of the damage done.

> Our natural instincts are not always the best things to follow when it comes to personal brand management.

Our posting on social media is not the only problem. Our dress, appearance, actions, social environments, and just about everything about us can be communicated by others through video (everyone has a video camera/phone in his pocket) or other forms of technology. Our brand is more public and more easily broadcast than at any other time in history. As technology increases, our personal brands will be more evident to others.

Technology is only part of the challenge. The accessibility of someone's past, present, and future sparks a desire in people to know this information. We have already seen that employers, schools, dates, and new acquaintances are frequently seeking out as much information about people as possible. This trend creates a stronger desire to access and know someone's brand either before they meet you or soon thereafter. Personal brand management is already important, but it will only become more important as technology and our culture continues to evolve. As you will see in the chapters that follow, this increased awareness will place greater importance on our spoken words, our dress and appearance, and how we project ourselves. It is a new age. Branding has become personal.

What Personal Branding *Isn't*

If you're like many people, you're probably thinking, "All this is fine for some people, but I'm not interested in being a 'brand manager.'" The truth is that you already are one. Every time you speak up in a meeting (whether it's in the boardroom or at PTA night), send an email, post a photo or status update online, even pick out your outfit for the day, you're sending a message about who you are. Like it or not, we're "reading" these messages about each other all the time. Far too often, however, what others read isn't what we intended, because we tend not to be mindful enough of the signals we're sending out.

Perhaps ironically, personal branding sometimes gets a bad rap. When Patrick and I give talks on the subject, we're often met with at least a few skeptical faces in the crowd. Here's a sampling of the misconceptions about personal branding that we hear (and, we hope, will soon dispel), along with a simple explanation of why each one simply isn't true:

- **Personal branding is something only celebrities need to think about.** It's true that celebrities, CEOs, and other prominent individuals tend to manage their respective brands. After all, their visibility amplifies the importance of their every move.

One careless comment, tweet, "wardrobe malfunction," or inebriated indiscretion can seriously tarnish or even ruin their image. But what some of us "regular folks" don't realize is that the same applies in our own lives. If you think these gaffes and missteps don't have an effect on how others see you, we've got a bridge to sell you. (More on brand damage, and ways to repair it, later in the book.)

- **Personal branding means you're self-absorbed. Only a selfish person would focus on how other people perceive her.** This one is a bit harder to respond to, because it requires a bit of introspection. If you truly don't care how others perceive you, then . . . there's no need to read on. But who among us doesn't want to be perceived as the best version of themselves? Who doesn't want to receive the respect and high regard of others, and be seen for who we really are? Strong personal branding isn't self-serving. It's goal-serving. Whatever your goal is, your personal brand will help you get there.

> Strong personal branding isn't self-serving. It's goal-serving.

- **Personal branding is manipulative.** In a perfect world, our actions would speak for themselves. There would be no misunderstandings, no noise interfering with the signals we're sending, and justice would always prevail. (Your favorite beverage would be flowing from every drinking fountain—let's not forget that part, either.) Since we don't live in a perfect world, it's important to be mindful of how our behavior is perceived. We can't control our image 100 percent, but why not make an effort to control it as much as we can? As I say in my talks, personal branding is only manipulative if it's used for negative purposes. Spreading untruths? Misrepresenting yourself or others? That's manipulative. Walking your talk, and putting your best foot forward (and shining your shoes first)? Not manipulative at all. It's that simple.

- **Personal branding is a form of lying.** Again, we're not suggesting you lie. In fact, we strongly suggest you don't. Rather, personal branding is about showing the world your authentic self—your best self—with clarity and purpose.

"Just Be Yourself" and Other Advice You Should Ignore

Remember Mom's advice to "Just be yourself"? I do—and I've decided to ignore it. I suggest you do, too. In a perfect world, this advice would work. No one would ever be misunderstood, and everyone would be seen in the best possible light. We would always give others the benefit of the doubt (and they would afford us the same respect in return).

But as we all know, we don't live in a perfect world. Rather, we live in a hectic, fast-paced, competitive, skeptical, even cynical world. In today's competitive job market, for example, employers are often looking for a reason to say no. Don't give them one. Your clothes, your words, your demeanor, and more all send a message, and that message should be consistent with your brand. Instead of "Just be yourself," I would suggest "Just be your best self"—or perhaps, "Always remember your brand."

Some other supposedly good advice comes to mind, as well. Here are a few old chestnuts, which I suggest you "un-follow":

- **"If someone doesn't like me, that's his problem."** Actually, if you're looking for a job, working toward a promotion, or trying to achieve any other goal in your life, the problem someone has with you is often going to be yours, not his. I'm not suggesting you abandon your principles, parrot what you think other people want you to hear, or masquerade as someone you're not. But keep in mind that we form opinions about each other constantly, and we do have some influence over how we're perceived. Making an effort can make all the difference.

- **"The cream always rises to the top."** This is another one you've probably heard over the years. The implication is that the best talent will always prevail. I don't know if that's true or not. But why leave it to fate? Putting your best foot forward is a better strategy than hoping you'll be seen as "the cream."

- **"Everything happens for a reason."** This one is invoked in many different types of circumstances. As with the previous example, I don't know if it's true. And I'm guessing you don't, either. Regardless of your beliefs on the subject, life experience has taught most of us that focus and effort are rewarded. These seem like pretty good "reasons" to me.

- **"I don't care what people think of me."** This is usually something someone says as they are thinking about work, neighbors, or general public. I would suggest, however, that most of us do care what some people think. Maybe it is your kids, spouse, neighbor, parents, future boss, or future relationship partner. It would be truly rare for someone to absolutely not care about what anyone thinks of her. If this describes you, you probably don't need this book. But your position might be worth a second look.

You're Already Soaking in It

The heading from this section probably dates me, since it comes from a TV ad that was popular in the 1970s. Not great for my youthful brand, perhaps. But the point here is that you might think you don't have a brand, and that you don't need one. But the truth is that like it or not, you already have one. When your name comes up, the people in your life think of something. You're smart. Quick with a funny comeback. Great with numbers. More reliable than a Swiss watch. (Or always the only one who got "stuck in traffic.") A great listener. A tireless partier. And so on. In addition, people who don't know you (or don't know you well), are looking you up online. What they see forms a first impression, just as it would in person. Your brand is out there. Whether—and how—you shape it is up to you.

So let's get started.

CHAPTER 2

Who Do You (and They) Think You Are?

Defining Your Personal Brand

Life isn't about finding yourself. Life is about creating yourself.

—George Bernard Shaw

To Be Or . . .

As we've already pointed out, each one of us has a personal brand. It starts when we're little. "Sara is the smart one." "Jack is great at soccer." "Steven is going places—he'll probably be president someday." When we were kids, we couldn't always influence or even understand the ways we were being "branded" (though there are certainly things that young people can do to maintain their personal brands; more on that in Chapter 9). My daughters and I discuss their brands on a regular basis, and it's become a positive and empowering part of our family culture. As we get older, we're not only more fully able to influence how others see us—our success in life, however we define it, depends on it.

Whatever you're hoping to achieve—making a sale, finding a

mate, getting into the college or training program of your dreams, earning a promotion, getting your novel published, raising a family in accordance with your values and priorities—whatever gets you up in the morning will be helped or hampered—and perhaps determined altogether—by the state of your personal brand.

Brand Creation in . . . Thirty Seconds

In eleventh grade, my high school philosophy teacher told our class, "People will spend the first thirty seconds when they meet you forming an opinion about you. Then they will spend the future of their relationship with you trying to find evidence to support their initial opinions." This was probably the beginning of my desire to manage my personal brand. As I grew older and went into professional sports and sales, I spent years working on perfecting this concept. While always being true to myself, and being careful to not develop a "fake" or "sales-y" persona, I was proactive in managing people's first perception of me. My wardrobe was mostly purchased based on how I wanted people to initially think of me. I practiced my thirty-second commercials, worked on voice quality, and made certain it matched that of a trusted adviser in strength, confidence, and tone. Bottom line, I wanted to manage what people thought of me in the beginning of our relationship. This would allow people to focus on my products, intellectual property, or advice, as opposed to attributes that distracted from my sales proposition. Managing what people think about me in that first impression has worked very well for me (not that I have always done it perfectly).

What people think of you will influence decisions to buy from you, spend time with you, work for or with you, listen to you, or even have a relationship with you. Managing the first thirty seconds of a relationship is one of the most powerful brand management strategies in existence.

It is an unfortunate reality though. I can't imagine that everyone is correct in his or her thirty-second evaluation of someone. So we have a real challenge to make sure we were lucky enough to influence people the way we wanted to in those first thirty seconds.

Patrick and I were working with a class of very diverse young executives in a personal branding exercise. We wanted to prove to them that even in a world where political correctness seemed to be improving, people would create perceptions quickly and possibly permanently.

Patrick put together a PowerPoint presentation with sixteen different images of people. These images had people in different types of dress, with different facial expressions, and behaving differently (one woman was attempting to handle a very disorganized stack of paper while juggling her purse).

We gave the class eight seconds per picture to decide the following and score each person on a scale of 1 to 10 (1 being Low and 10 being High). Would they purchase something from them? Do they trust them? Would they consider them a potential trusted adviser? Do they like them?

The results were very interesting. They all picked the same three people as the top scored people, based on dress, posture, fitness level, and modern (not too modern) styles. What I found to be more interesting was that not *one* person in the class said "I can't make these decisions in eight seconds or less." Yes, they were comfortable making judgment decisions about people based on an immediate evaluation of their appearance. This is because we do this naturally. Some people will read this and believe it is a terrible thing. Terrible or not, Patrick and I have done this exercise with more than two hundred people, in all types of environments. The results are always the same, and the people have never said they couldn't do it or were uncomfortable with the exercise.

Our brands are quickly defined and difficult to revise. You have the choice to help influence what others think of you. It will only work if you are proactive as opposed to reactive.

Brand Creation in . . . Four Minutes

In July 2008, my wife invited a new friend and her husband over for dinner. I had not met them prior to this dinner, so I figured the evening would be more interesting if I did a little research on them before they arrived. I searched Google and Ask.com and found articles, work history, and various other bits of information about each of them within about four minutes of research. I was so proud and impressed with how good I was going to be in conversations. I was bragging to my wife about how I was going to be crafty with my questions and conversations topics.

The couple arrived, and we began to get to know each other. I was thinking about how I would begin to introduce conversations based on my research when the guy said, "Larry, I was looking you up online this afternoon, and I was impressed with what I saw."

Now what would I do? My game was ruined. I couldn't dance around the fact that I had looked him up, as well. I had to fess up.

> People will spend about four minutes learning about you via your Internet footprint prior to meeting you.

"That is so funny," I responded. "I looked you up today, as well. I saw you caught a big tarpon." That's all I had. My brilliant strategy turned into a simple, dumb statement. That moment, however, became the beginning of a new realization in personal brand management. People will spend about four minutes learning about you via your Internet footprint prior to meeting you.

In the years since this dinner, researching and predetermining thought development have clearly become the norm. This is especially true when it comes to business relationships. Since this event, I have been told many times that I have been "looked up." Regarding this "minus four minutes," it is important to recognize that your brand precedes your physical presence. Your footprint on the Internet will include pictures, videos, articles about you, articles or blogs you have written, social media content, and comments others may have made about you. Some of you think, Ha! This doesn't apply to me. You can't find anything about me on the Internet.

First, it is easy to find information about people online. It doesn't take much effort to find the price of a house, someone's estimated income, a Social Security number, a driver's license number, credit history, marriage information, an address, and much more. Second, if people's presence is limited online, they will be considered "old school" and not up to speed with what the world is doing. That was okay in a world where it took a full generation to evolve how we interacted or did business. But in a world that changes daily, if someone wants to be considered relevant, it is important to manage a brand online and off.

We will address how to maximize your footprint in Chapter 4. It is critical, however, to manage your "minus four minutes."

Brand Creation in . . . Two Years

Patrick has continually hounded—I mean, gently encouraged—me to write blogs, create online videos, write articles, and connect with others online. He set up my website and our company websites. He has optimized our entire online footprint to maximize control of what people find when they look us up. (You'll find more on how to optimize your Internet presence in Chapter 4.)

I have worked extensively in the insurance industry over the past few years—it's not a cutting-edge industry when it comes to technology and Internet usage. Recently, in the space of one day, I spoke with two different CEOs of insurance agencies, one in South Carolina and the other in Minnesota, about the prospect of entering a business relationship. In each of these discussions, the CEO informed me that it was not necessary to give any introduction or background about myself because he had already been reading my articles, blogs, and websites, along with my LinkedIn page and other information, for the past two years. My brand was established as a trusted and respected consultant/ adviser prior to the calls. He was already looking for advice and my intellectual property when we started the call. This new opportunity of proactive brand management is changing and speeding up the sales process, as well as creating opportunities that didn't exist before.

Most people in the professional sales arena have a huge hurdle to jump when it comes to being trusted and perceived as credible. They have to spend time early in the sales process creating credibility and a brand that gives the perception that they should be heard and believed, and that they are capable. What if they didn't have to do that? What if their brand preceded them? What if buyers believed they were credible long before they arrived? How would that change how they sell? How would that impact the speed of selling? The answers to these questions are being seen in the positive results from salespeople who are proactively managing their respective brands. Many of the salespeople I coach are walking in the door as true, trusted advisers, because the buyer already sees them as credible and worthy. It changes everything.

Not Just for Seasoned Pros

Brand management isn't reserved for seasoned sales veterans alone. The message of proactively differentiating yourself described above can be implemented by young, inexperienced people, as well.

Patrick frequently ran classes that taught young salespeople how to become true professionals. One of the main hurdles that most of these rookies faced was creating perceived value. He taught them different strategies to combat the reality of their youth. One of these was to fully embrace technology. If they were willing to purposefully manage their brand, provide valuable content (e.g., via blog posts and other commentary on market issues), and utilize technology to connect, then they had a distinct advantage over some of their market sector's seasoned professionals.

If a rookie had a purposefully managed brand and her competitor did not, she would go into a prospect meeting with a leg up right off the bat! As we know, her prospect was most likely going to search for her online prior to the meeting. If the rookie's search results came back positive and powerful, and her competitor was old, outdated, or even nonexistent, this was certainly beneficial for her. These differentiation strategies don't apply just online.

One of the most powerful and effective stories of offline brand management that Patrick ever encountered was that of a young insurance producer in Florida. This producer fully understood the power of personal branding and the idea of "birds of a feather flocking together" (which we will address in Chapter 5). He knew he didn't have years of experience and results to sell, so he looked for another way to get noticed by decision makers.

This young producer was only a few years out of college and was still a huge supporter of his school's football team. He donated enough money to be at the top level of the university's booster club (something he saw as an investment in himself, more than a donation or expense), which allowed him access to the luxury suites at games. Instead of tailgating and hanging out with his buddies, this producer made a bold move by becoming the youngest member of the elite level inside the booster club. Just as Patrick has created positive buzz with my online branding, this young producer did the same with his involvement in the booster club. Yes, his reputation preceded him, and it was very positive.

Don't Get Lost in Translation

Despite our best efforts, we are often misunderstood. We think (or simply hope) we're being perceived a certain way, when in fact we are not. In many instances, we don't even know we're being misunderstood. We haven't invited feedback, or we haven't been attuned to it. Perhaps we've chosen to ignore it. From a branding standpoint, feedback is essential—soliciting it, paying attention to it, and even anticipating it so that we can avoid misperceptions before they're formed in the first place.

I have to manage this issue frequently. I am an introvert. Many public speakers are introverts, despite what most people might think. We seem so outgoing on the stage, but we are actually comfortable because we are alone up there, in control of our own words but not interacting much with others. But when we leave the podium, people are often surprised, and disappointed, that we are not as lively in one-on-one interactions. Our energy level and passion seem diminished.

A man admitted to me a while back that he didn't like me very much when he first met me. He had seen me speak and thought that I would be a dynamic personality who was lively and interactive. He came up to me and found me to be reserved and quiet. He interpreted my behavior as not liking him and thinking I was "too good for him." Nothing could be further from the truth. Over time, this person has become a dear friend and knows me well. He recently told me he can't believe he ever thought those negative things about me because he sees me as humble, giving, and focused on others. I was mortified when I heard his original thoughts. I can see, however, how my behaviors sent the message of a very negative brand.

Like it or not, the perceptions we create with our behaviors will determine our brand. Remember that everyone you interact with (one-on-one, in a group setting, or online) is filtering her perceptions of you through her own unique lens, informed by her own concerns, biases, insecurities, and more. How she perceives your brand will be determined not just by what she thinks of you, but how she feels about you.

So what are some commonly misunderstood qualities?

Intelligent: know-it-all
Authoritative: bossy or arrogant
Inquisitive: nosy
Attractive: stuck-up or vain
Good results: teachers', bosses', or coaches' pet
Quiet: standoffish, superior

I'm not suggesting you quit being you. Rather, I'm reminding you that even positive traits and good intentions can be misunderstood—and often are. So it's wise to try to manage those misperceptions through other behaviors.

Back to my being an introvert and being misunderstood. I have used a few techniques to try to overcome this negative perception. I tell people I am an introvert whenever I get an opportunity. This helps a lot. Many times this gives people a chance to poke fun at me and make our time together more comfortable. I will also tell people that I am not good at working entire rooms of people and I ask them to please come up to me because it is very valuable for me to get time with each person. I have also learned to be very present in every relationship. This gives the person confidence that he is important to me.

I don't know that I will ever perfect this strategy, but I know it is critical to my success in managing my brand.

I believe all of us have certain behaviors and traits that can be misunderstood. Be introspective, and honest with yourself. Then think of creative ways to manage the misperception, so that you can provide more clarity to others about who you really are.

Here are some examples:

Smart or intelligent: know-it-all—Be a great listener and seek to understand before seeking to be understood.

Authoritative: bossy—Sell your ideas versus telling your ideas to people. That means listening to others and offering examples of why you are making certain decisions.

Inquisitive: nosy—Give explanations as to why you are asking questions.

Attractive: better than others—Be present in relationships and make others the focus of your conversations.

Good results: pet—Give credit to others and share the credit/ rewards where appropriate.

Quiet: think you are too good for others—Smile, ask questions to get others talking, maintain good eye contact.

Be creative and think about how you can prevent others' misperceptions from the start.

Seven Steps to a Great Brand

Brand creation and management need to be purposeful and consistent. It is not a one-time event, and it will evolve throughout your life. The planning process looks at your current situation, its potential, and its future, and then lays out specific steps to get you there. The following steps are one path to develop and manage your brand:

Step 1: Write down what you believe people think of you today. Make sure to write down all of the positive, negative, and neutral items that come to mind. Ask others to give you information, as well. Be careful, however: They may not tell you everything you need to know. You will clearly get the positive things. The negative things will be the hardest to extract. If you have very close friends, ask them to be brutally honest and let you know what others think of you. If you have the ability to get anonymous feedback from people in your work environment, that can be helpful, too.

Examples: Hardworking, disciplined, intelligent, calm, caring, philanthropic, hardheaded, tough, approachable, and high-risk.

Step 2: Think about your future. Determine your goals in life: career, family, legacy, etc. What brand items will help you get there faster and ensure that you reach them? Write down the characteristics you'll need to have in order to maximize your chances of reaching your goals. Will you need to be perceived as intelligent? Would it benefit you to be thought of as honest or hardworking? Are you a problem solver or researcher? Are you detailed, focused, and kind? At what do you excel? What value do you bring to relationships? Try looking at industry leaders, successful people, mentors, or those whom you look up to. What items do you see? Can you emulate some of them? Look to those who are ahead of you in your organization, at school, etc. What items do you see? What items do others see?

Be as specific as possible, keeping your long-term goals in mind. It's also important to note whether your brand's characteristics are too similar to everyone else's. Being friendly, hardworking, and tech-savvy are not unique. Most people could say the same things about themselves. The idea here is to set yourself apart from the rest of the pack. If your company has a specific set of values, it would be a good idea to include those in your brand (see Chapter 7 for more on individuals within the corporate brand).

Examples: Intelligent, problem solver, creative, innovative, honest, disciplined, detailed, focused, results oriented, etc.

Step 3: Do a gap analysis. What is the difference between your brand today (your answer from Step 1) and your desired brand (your answer from Step 2)? This is the hard part. Your objective here is to get clarity on what needs to be changed or developed in order to reach your desired brand. Simply list what is the same and what is different.

Example: Items that are on the second list but not the first: problem solver, creative, innovative, honest, detailed, focused, and results oriented.

Step 4: Develop action items to build a new brand (or eliminate old brand items). To effectively manage your brand, you need to be purposeful in everything you do, ensuring that you are communicating a consistent brand message.

Example: Innovative—start bringing some ideas to meetings, and be prepared to sell those ideas. Don't be protective of new innovations and ideas. Let people know what I am thinking. Let people know I research new ideas and am very creative.

Step 5: Identify where and how you will project your brand. Realize that dress, style, what type of car you drive, voice tone and quality, friends, recreation, weight, health, social environments, where you live, language you use, what subjects you reference in conversations, and social media postings all have an influence on your brand. Think about the types of conversations you will need to have in order to make a positive impact on what people will think of when they think of you. Become purposeful about what you post on social media sites and when you post it, and always ask, "How will this impact my brand?"

Example: Innovative—get in front of leaders and managers with my new ideas more often. Also, share new ideas with clients to get their feedback and input on the value of those ideas. Make sure to package my ideas effectively and polish my presentation in order to showcase them as high value.

Step 6: List what you must do to protect your brand. This is one of the most critical steps. I have seen people blow their brand because of not thinking this step through. Should you never drink in public? Should you not talk publicly (or not too much) about a certain aspect of your life? Should you always dress a certain way to get people to think a certain way about you? Make sure to identify any way your brand could be damaged, and put rules and systems in place to protect your brand.

Example: Innovative—don't discuss or present ideas in depth without first thinking through them and having confidence they will work. Poor ideas that are not well thought out will damage my brand in terms of innovation.

Step 7: Rinse and repeat. Every six months, review Steps 1 through 6. Your brand will change and evolve. Stay on it. Use the Brand Assessment Worksheet at the end of the book for reference.

Don't get too caught up in details and let them bog you

> Bottom line: be proactive in brand identification and management. It *will* make a difference.

down. The keys are to identify what you want your brand to be, and act accordingly. These details will help you refine and perfect your brand. Bottom line: be proactive in brand identification and management. It *will* make a difference.

Harness the Power of "Always"

"Always" statements are a method I use to help our clients and my team to define, in specific terms, who they are or who they want to be. The concept allows you to create a clear mental picture of your brand. The concept is simple: What are five specific things you pride yourself on doing regularly? (You might not literally "always" do them, but that would be ideal.) These are activities and habits that are not just routine; they're also important to you. They help define what matters to you most. If possible, mention why you do each one. What value does it add to your brand—and to your interactions with others?

Here are some of my "always" statements:

I always look my kids in the eye when we're talking. It shows that I am a dad who cares about what they have to say.

I always dress "half up" when in any environment where I want to be noticed or be seen as an adviser. (For more information on dressing "half up," see page 41.)

I always take the time to read up on matters in my field and on current events, because I want to be respected for being intelligent and well read.

I always "open new files," or bring up new concepts when I speak to people, so they can see me as a thought leader.

I always am present with my wife and kids and do not allow myself to be distracted with technology or external thoughts when I'm with them, so that they will know my focus is truly on our time together.

These statements are more than just a one-time exercise. They can become an important touchstone when it comes to staying connected to your desired brand. After all, your brand is only as strong as your behavior, on a daily and even moment-to-moment basis. "Always" statements can help keep you—and your brand—on track. Think of them as goals to strive for every day.

> Your brand is only as strong as your behavior, on a daily and even moment-to-moment basis.

When I work with my staff of advisers on managing their brands, we agree on certain "always" statements to maintain focus. Some of those are:

We always:

. . . "Open new files" when we speak.

. . . Seek to understand before seeking to be understood.

. . . Stay present in the moment, and make the person we are talking to feel she is the only client that matters.

This works for individual brands, family brands, and corporate brands. Give it a try and see for yourself.

Finding (and Using) Your Voice

Your voice can be a very high-impact part of your brand. I don't believe it is the most important piece of someone's brand. It can, however, be something that creates brand opportunity or brand damage.

The positives usually occur when the voice clearly matches the desired brand. If you desire to have a soft, mature, and kind brand, you would want a voice tone that matches. If you desire to be known as the disciplined and intense football coach, you should have a booming, powerful voice. These types of examples are usually not where we find ourselves coaching people on voice. The opportunity is where we have people who have conflicting voice tone, volume, or speech patterns.

When a big guy has a high-pitched voice or a young person is overly loud, we see potential brand damage. We realize some tone and voice quality issues are genetic and can't be changed, but we have seen improvements with voice coaches and practice.

As mentioned above, this isn't the most important part of brand management. But I do have a few suggestions for rounding out your brand by being mindful of your speech patterns:

- **Tone**—Tone is one of the hardest items to change. As mentioned above, a voice coach can help improve the tone to be a higher quality and one that moves toward your desired brand. A voice coach can also help give you honest feedback as to the perception of your voice as others might experience it.

- **Language**—Your brand is clearly expressed by the type of language you use. One of my early mentors told me that curse words were a substitution for intelligence and creativity. Now don't get me wrong, I have heard some pretty creative cursing in my life. That advice stuck with me, however. I realized it *could* sound ignorant if I chose to use curse words in place of more creative adjectives. On the other hand, I was at a training program recently with a large group of very young executives. One of the executives was clearly trying to show how smart he was. He used words that were very uncommon with this crowd. He was trying to speak over their heads so he could look smart. He missed the boat on this attempt. Everyone I spoke to referred to him as pompous and arrogant. So, using words that make you look overly intelligent or ignorant aren't right or wrong. The key is to have the right language choices that will give a clear message of what you want people to think of you.

- **Volume**—This is an area where many people don't realize they are impacting their brand. I like the "Goldilocks" method here. Don't be too loud or too soft. Your voice should blend into any situation as just right. Overly loud people are branded as obnoxious and lacking self-control. People who speak too softly to be heard are branded as timid and weak. This is another place where a session or two with a voice coach could be helpful. He will be honest with you and give you good feedback on the right volume.

- **Articulation**—You want to be clear and understood when you speak. When my wife was pregnant with our first child, we went to a baseball game. The announcer was hard to understand as he slurred a lot of his words. He was trying to be cute in his style. As a pregnant woman she was having a lot of food cravings; I clearly understood this was normal. At one of the breaks between innings, the announcer came on the loudspeaker and said, "Look in your program on page 34. If you have a black mark on the page, you are a winner. Just come up to the press box and get your prize." My wife jumped up and asked me for my program. She said, "Fries, you win fries. I want fries! Look on that page, *now*!" Again, the announcer was not very clear . . . and maybe she was going to hear what she wanted to hear. This announcer, however, was frustrating to all attendees (not just the pregnant ones). I have heard others attempt to get cute with their speaking style. It can work, but it is essential that you clearly articulate your words.

- **Frequency**—This one is my favorite. My dad used to say "You can be silent and thought a fool or open your mouth and remove all doubt." I only wish I would have taken this advice more often in my life. Yes, this one also falls in the "Goldilocks" category. The frequency with which you speak needs to be "just right." People who talk too much and people who talk too little will both get negative brands. Have you ever spoken to someone who just looks at you and won't respond or give feedback? That is rough and not very attractive. And we all know the impact of someone who consistently talks too much.

These are just guidelines, not hard-and-fast rules. It all comes back to what you want people to think of you. If you want to be seen as someone who talks a lot and is the life of every party, well, you know what to do. My challenge is to observe these aspects of your speech and determine if you are sending the brand message you desire.

Making Presentations Count

It has been said that one of the biggest fears humans have is to speak in public. I have never had that issue. As a matter of fact, my wife says my biggest fear is to not have an audience to speak to.

Whether you fear speaking or love it, realize it is an incredible opportunity to communicate your personal brand.

I do a lot of presentation skills training and speechwriting for clients. I always ask the person I am working with to tell me what she wants the audience to think of her when she finishes speaking. I believe in the theory that people won't necessarily

> People won't necessarily remember what you say, but they will remember how you made them feel.

remember what you say, but they will remember how you made them feel. I also believe you will leave them with a perception of your brand.

How many times have you left a speech and remarked to someone what you thought of the speaker? In doing that, you have expressed your opinion of his or her brand.

When you speak, you can take control of your brand with that audience. You can tell them what you want them to think of you. The technique is simple. Define what you want the audience to think and make sure to incorporate that into your speech through direct and indirect messaging, and avoid being misunderstood.

Direct Messaging

Tell them what you want them to believe. Many times in speeches I have stated, "I have a passion for helping orphans." Now, the purpose may be to get them to participate with me in supporting orphans or simply to understand where I am coming from on a topic. But, for whatever reason at that time, I want it to be clear what I need them to think about me. Statements like "I grew up learning a good work ethic," or "Education is important to me," are ways of simply telling your audience something about you that you want them to know.

Indirect Messaging

Use statements or stories that reflect on your brand. My team of advisers are all known as thought leaders, an important brand trait for us to have as business advisers. Before every speech they make, they are required to tell me what new ideas they will introduce in their speech. It has to be a new concept, a new way of looking at something, new packaging of ideas, or something that introduces something new to the audience. Now, they are not saying, "I am a thought leader." My experience, however, is that most of the time our audiences respond to our speeches by stating the information was "thought leadership." Message delivered.

Avoid Being Misunderstood

Unfortunately, public speakers are often misunderstood. They give speeches to communicate information to others. They don't think about their message as a way of expressing their brand. As a result, the audience walks away thinking things about them that might not be accurate—for example, that they're pretentious (too much jargon use), arrogant (long-winded and self-focused), and so on. I was in the audience of a corporate speech a few years ago. The speaker communicated some very important pieces of information in a dry and long-winded manner. He had three good points that were critical to his message. He would have been a hero if he had communicated those three things and stepped down from the podium. He would have been seen as brilliant, articulate, and a clear communicator. As I walked out of the session, however, I overheard people saying things like, "He won't stop talking," and "I can't remember what he said, but I know I wouldn't listen to him speak again."

Try your best to anticipate the ways your presentation might be misinterpreted—and do your best to prevent the misperception before it happens.

DRESSING "HALF UP"

You might believe that "just be yourself" is good advice when it comes to deciding what to wear. If you're trying to bolster your personal brand, I have bad news for you. What you wear sends a signal to everyone you meet.

Our clothes send messages, whether we intend them to or not. Neat, serious, comfortable, careless, sloppy, confident, formal . . . these and many other messages are sent by our appearance.

Don't get me wrong; choosing clothes that are "too nice" for the situation can be a problem, too. Too formal, too fussy, too showy, too mature—these aren't good messages to send, either. So what's a brand-aware person to do? Here's a technique I recommend often. It's one that works well for me.

Whatever the recommended dress is for an event, I go "half up." An example would be wearing long dress slacks to play golf. I may wear a jacket over a dress shirt at a business casual event. You can usually just add a piece of clothing (or add length to clothing) to be "half up." For women, adding an accessory such as a nice scarf or piece of jewelry can do the trick. I find that the person dressed a little nicer usually represents someone in charge or in more of an advisory-level position. He tends to be respected a bit more and get recognized. Be careful though: dressing a full level up can put you out of place and

continued on next page . . .

---

send a message of inappropriateness or showing off. A half step up is usually just right.

A few common clothing gaffes that can damage your desired brand are:

- Wearing clothes that are outdated

- Looking wrinkled, disheveled, or unclean

- Dressing too casually ("half down") at an event—for example, wearing jeans when others are in more formal attire

- Showing inappropriate amounts of skin (this goes for both sexes)

CHAPTER 3

The Care and Feeding of Your Personal Brand

You can't build a reputation on what you are going to do.

—Henry Ford

My Brand: Maintained Over Time, Conveyed in a Few Moments

It's been said that it takes years to become an overnight success. The same is true when it comes to establishing a personal brand. Everyone wants to make a good first impression, but the truth is that a significant amount of forethought and daily maintenance are required to truly establish a personal brand. To borrow a gardening metaphor, you have to plant a lot of seeds, water and prune the plants, and remember to present a bouquet, too.

When I give talks about personal branding, I like to have a little fun with the audience. I ask them to write down what they think of me. Then I share with them some adjectives from my desired brand (which I keep on my iPad and review regularly). It is always rewarding to see the audience's amazement when I rattle off many of the words they have just jotted down. Some seem to think it's magic—but of course it isn't. Rather, it's mindful messaging on my part. In various ways, I have "told" them what to think. That is, I established my brand by giving them cues throughout my remarks.

Some items on my desired brand list include: intelligent, thought leader, disciplined, healthy and fit, and adoration for my family. How do I influence others to have these thoughts?

Intelligent. I reference other smart people frequently. I read a lot and refer to these books when teaching, speaking, and interacting with others. I read highly complex books and express opinions about them.

Thought leader. I write blog posts about current events, and make arguments that are new and challenging to my readers. My desire is to open new files in the minds of my audience every time I write, speak, or interact with others. I persuade rather than inform.

Disciplined. This is shown mostly through healthy eating, a lack of drinking in public, and physical fitness. I post items on my social media to highlight bike racing, workouts, and other health-related activities to let people know my level of seriousness regarding being physically fit.

Adoration for my wife and five daughters. I use social media for this area of brand management. I also refer to my girls in speeches and at events. A big public image makes me seem unapproachable at times, so it is important that I make myself real to others and allow them to see what I value the most.

These are some of the things I do to influence how others see me. I do other things, however, to protect my brand. I use much of my social media space to communicate the softer and approachable side of my personality. I constantly evaluate my clothes and how I dress for different events and activities. I use the model of "half up" in my dress (see page 41).

Patrick monitors my Internet presence on a daily basis to ensure others aren't damaging my brand and to make sure I haven't made any inadvertent missteps (i.e., done something stupid).

Recently I posted something on my Facebook page during my travels. It was misunderstood by a reader and he bashed my brand in comments. Patrick informed me within minutes of the post so that I could quickly address the perception. This type of monitoring can make all the difference. What this guy posted in response to my original post could have potentially damaged my brand in a big way.

Our family watches out for each other and makes sure we are projecting a proper family brand.

Brand management is full-time work. When you get it down, it becomes second nature and part of your everyday activi-

> Brand management is full-time work.

ties. It is comforting. There's probably nothing more frustrating than being misunderstood. Proper brand management increases the chance of being understood exactly the way you desire. Of course, you can't fully control how others see you—that will always be in the eye of the beholder—but careful brand management is a much wiser approach than letting your brand happen by chance.

It Takes a Village: Gathering a Team of Advisers

My adviser team is the strongest in the insurance and risk consulting business. They are experienced, intelligent, and intuitive, and they get results for their clients. We are always pushing each other to achieve excellence, in the particular ways each one of us defines it. I have learned a lot about personal branding from working with them. Here are a few of the key lessons they've helped me learn.

Constant Monitoring Pays Off

Every few months I ask my team, "What do you want people to think of when they think of you?" They have a few core things that never change. Some have brands that represent actual experience in the insurance business. Some have brands of being outstanding teachers. One of our advisers is known for being excellent in operations management. Another has a fantastic brand around hiring and HR evaluations. The more specific your personal brand is, the more successful you will be in keeping it strong. And the more often you monitor your brand, the more accurate and relevant it will be.

Your Brand Is a Moving Target

Change is inevitable, and happening all around us. In order to make an impact on others, and to continue to grow and reach our goals, our brands must evolve. One of my advisers has been including more examples of his studying and reading when he gives speeches, in order to demonstrate the increasing levels of knowledge he's striving to achieve. Another adviser has great sales skills but wants to grow into leadership roles. He makes sure to open discussions with clients in areas that are more focused on leadership and operations. This allows him the opportunity to strengthen his brand in this regard. Which side of your skill set you want to highlight will change and shift over time. What worked two years ago is probably in need of some revisiting today. (For age- and stage-specific strategies, see Chapter 9.) Successful brand management stays ahead of this curve. It is a process of constant reevaluation and revision.

Our Natural Instincts Can Steer Us Wrong—and Often Do

Personal brand management is not natural, and it isn't easy. When I check in with my advisers about our respective brands, we are often surprised at how purposeful we have to be to make sure we shape our image thoughtfully and purposely. If left to our instincts, we might do otherwise. We would likely revert to old habits, lean on outdated modes of communication, and otherwise undercut the impact we'd like to make. Assuming others will see through our quirks, relying on sarcasm or other questionable forms of "humor," letting our social media profiles languish—these are all common mistakes that many of us will fall into without purposeful care and maintenance of our brands.

Preparation Is Everything

One way I have helped my team members shape their brands is to prepare them for events. If we have a meeting with clients, prior to the event they are required to articulate (to me) how they will influence what people think of them. Some of the preparation might seem minor or micromanaging. But the truth is that it's quite the opposite. Realizing you're in control of much of how you're perceived is empowering. How you introduce yourself, handle routine things like introductions and seating, and make presentations (whether formal or otherwise) are all opportunities to shape how others perceive you. My team members have become very skilled at identifying these opportunities and maximizing them. Thinking these moments through in advance can truly yield strong results.

Course Corrections Won't
Happen on Their Own

One of my team members has a very strong background in operations and smaller business sales. She is known in Canada as one of the most experienced and knowledgeable advisers in these areas. Over the past twenty years, she has worked hard to expand her skills and knowledge in many areas, including finance, sales, and CEO-level advising. As a matter of fact, she is one of the people to whom I now go to for advice on these issues.

So what's the problem? Her brand as a go-to leader in operations issues preceded her. She had become, in some ways, "a victim of her own success." When clients and others in the industry approached her, they went directly to operations and small-business issues, and were visibly uncomfortable when she tried to introduce her other areas of expertise. She was letting others direct the conversation, and thereby giving up control of her own brand.

In order to address the problem, I worked with her to develop some new strategies, including:

- Crafting conversation starters associated with her desired skill areas and strengths

- Starting conversations instead of letting others start them

- Speaking, writing, and blogging on topics directly related to the new brand items

- Minimizing her emphasis on the old brand items

- Referring questions about old brand items to a trusted colleague who is working on those elements of his or her brand.

This plan worked well. Over a two-year period, she moved her brand closer to these desired items. Her next challenge was her internal team (the other advisers). They continued to feed her all of the operations consulting work, and they were sending a brand message that she is "the operations person." So she and I communicated her desired brand to them. We gave them examples of her strengths and unique knowledge in many areas of leadership, finance, sales, and CEO-level management. We proactively managed how they would influence her brand, as well, by giving them new ways to deal with the operations items versus sending them to her. This was a great lesson for me: realizing that we can proactively manage our brand by identifying what we want people to think and purposefully manage the key touch points with those we want to influence. But we may have to have others help us, as well. Our family, friends, and colleagues have an influence on our brand. We need to give them clarity about our brand so they don't damage it. They can help you revise your image, and they can also help keep you accountable to follow through on your words and intentions.

"Can't I Outsource It?"

I get this question a lot when I give presentations on the importance of personal brand management. The short answer is yes . . . sort of.

As with everything about personal brand management, the area of outsourcing is changing rapidly. At the moment, an individual can pay less than $200 a month to get a college student to manage her brand for her. One company paid a university a small donation to the marketing department to have a project team (students) develop the initial website, blogs, video blogs, and individual brand pages on all its employees. This was very effective and very low-cost solution. As long as a company has a very clear plan for managing the corporate and individual brands, and good guidelines for each, a lot of talented young people out there can do a great job of managing and monitoring the brand. It is still a good idea to have someone with good strategic brand management skills monitor the process and maintain regular reviews.

On the other hand, *be careful*. Someone just making posts and adding content can hurt you. Make sure you have complete clarity on what you want to accomplish; that may require professional help. We have seen inexperienced people trying to manage individual brands, and it has resulted in big brand damage. One executive let his high school daughter manage his social media and online presence. She posted so many things every day for him that he ended up getting a brand of being on social media too much. His clients thought he wasn't working and was spending all his time in a social media addiction. A good strategy and guidelines are a must-have in personal brand management—whether you're carrying out the plan yourself or hiring someone else to help you manage and execute it.

As long as you have a good plan and it is clear what you want to accomplish, this low-cost strategy can work well for you. Just don't allow a lot of freedom. Students and interns don't always have enough business experience to determine good judgment. Keep tight reins on them. Listen to their ideas, and encourage them to be creative. Just make sure you see it before the creativity hits the public.

The next option is to hire an outside firm to manage your corporate and personal brands. This strategy is a very touchy subject for me to address. The problem with a large number of professional marketing firms is that they can rob you blind by doing a lot of activity (posts, pictures, blogs, tweets, etc.) and getting you zero results. Companies will show you tons of activity, including site-hit activity, and can generate reports that make you feel really good. The results you want, however, are more sales, increased brand awareness, and proactive brand management prior to a salesperson visiting a client, to name a few.

I have seen businesses write big checks and get nothing in return. A company called me recently to tell me about its amazing new social media strategy and online technology presence. They had spent $160,000 on a website, full strategic social media marketing plan, blogging setup, individual brands created on the website, social media setup, and a six-month management program. It had been about three months into the program, so I went and looked around. It was pretty! Wow, they had a beautiful, stagnant website. It was a $160,000 brochure and a bunch of posts (blogs, social media pushes, etc.). In three months, however, they had six followers—all of whom were employees of the company. Patrick and I could have helped them get a better setup for no more than $25,000 and had thousands of followers with a more focused plan.

The best advice I can give is to ask a company to show you measurable results they have brought prior clients. Don't let them sell you based on what they "could" do for you. Make sure you talk to the companies with whom they have worked and verify the quantifiable results. "We are popular and get a lot of hits" is not good enough. A lot of games can be played in this arena. Get measurements that are clearly turning into sales, profits, and desired outcomes. Also, make sure they have a plan to manage individual brands in the company, as well. It all has to fit together.

I believe this game is going to get clearer very soon. So many people are starting to see such clear results from good social media and technology strategies in managing company and individual brands that surely we will soon be getting blueprints of success that can be followed. It is my prediction that every business-to-business company will have an (full- or part-time) internal brand manager by 2015.

Brand Management 101

Now that you've decided what your desired brand is and learned a bit about how to proactively manage your image, how do you keep yourself on track? After all, a personal brand exists in other people's opinions and regard. It's what they think of you. So how can you maintain your brand while also evolving with the times?

> A personal brand exists in other people's opinions and regard.

Keep Asking Why

Patrick has a very successful way of keeping a brand sharp and relevant. He explains that most people who have spent time around young children know the "why" stage. This typically happens around three years old. During this highly frustrating time (for parents), children begin to question everything. They not only question the ways of the world but also every statement that they hear. The questioning isn't designed to intentionally annoy everyone around them; it's more a genuine interest in why things are the way they are. They also want to know why they have to do what they are told. Luckily for parents, they grow out of this phase; however, when this stage is over, something is lost, too. As we grow older, we lose some of that curiosity that we once had. We begin to conform and stop challenging with "Why?"

As you develop your plan, continue to ask yourself "Why?" Challenge your brand, challenge your brand items, and challenge your plan.

Use Media to Your Advantage

As Patrick has taught me, media can refer to any communication portal—the Internet, traditional media outlets, websites, images, video, and more. Media should be seen as one way to manage your personal brand, not the only way. Not all of your brand's items fall under media. Of course, this is still a very important piece. Some questions to consider here are:

- Are you easy to find?

This is especially important if you have a common name or company name. For example, if your name is Joe Smith or Jane Doe, it will be much harder for someone to find the Joe that someone is looking for. It could be very damaging if someone is looking for you but finds the wrong Joe.

- Do you have a good defense in place to monitor your brand? (We will cover this in detail in the next section.)

- Do you have consistency in the message across all media?

Your brand message needs to be consistent. Look to incorporate a standard tagline or bio, profile picture, brand items, etc.

- Is media enhancing, or damaging, your brand?

- Do pictures, videos, and other media portray the brand that you are trying to convey? For example, if you are looking to be viewed as a leader with strong morals, it would probably be very damaging to have pictures surface of you at a gentleman's club.

Social Media

We are all social by nature. The genius of what social media platforms do is that it allows us to relate, connect, and network the way we always have; these applications just make it easier. Social media includes blogging and conversations, the well-known Facebook, Twitter, and LinkedIn, as well as other social platforms like Google+, Pinterest, etc. Some items to consider with social media are:

- Are you using these platforms to enhance your brand message?

- Is there consistency in the powerful message across all social media?

- Are you a proactive communicator or passive listener?

- Are your profiles up to date, error-free, and clearly communicated? It should be easy to see where you go to school or work. It should be easy to identify what you do, what you like, and what you stand for. Your profiles should also be free of grammar and spelling errors. Just because it's online doesn't mean that it is okay to be sloppy with language.

Brand Maintenance: Your Digital Marketing Strategy

You should revisit your brand every few months to account for change. Even if you would like to keep your brand's characteristics the same, perhaps you would like to enhance one of them. Or maybe a new tool has come into play to help you manage your brand. Below is a simple blueprint to ensure that you have a proactive approach to maintaining your brand online.

Who?

Know your audience. The key starting point for any strategy is to ask the following questions: To whom are you trying to appeal? Are you looking to connect with clients or prospects, or both? Are you looking for a job, seeking out employees, or looking for a date? Who is your demographic? Digital presence and social media allow you to target specific groups in a way that was never possible offline. The best strategies are built on specific target markets, so you need to decide whom to target before you figure out how to do it.

Do you have a branding team? Assess your team's strengths in the following categories:

- **Leadership (this better be you).** You must be the ultimate decision maker on your personal brand. Yes, you can build a team and have others manage some of the necessary functions, but you still have to control the process.

- **Content.** Blogging and content creation are keys to any marketing program today. The same goes with a personal branding strategy. Your content can be original posts or comments, reposting, or discussing current world or industry events. It could also be videos, songs, etc. If you aren't wired to sit down and write content, then you should consider either hiring someone to help you or finding creative ways to engage in conversations online.

- **Creativity/graphics.** This is a higher-end item but something to consider. Especially in the social media world, having an aesthetically pleasing profile and website/blog is important. Having a personal logo or brand identity and a professional-looking website/blog, and creating infographics and other items may be a bit too much if you are just starting your personal branding approach, but they are things to consider.

- **Technology.** As we've discussed, technology can be overwhelming. It can certainly enhance your brand, but it brings with it a lot of complexity as well. Having someone on your team who understands current and emerging technologies will greatly help. He or she should be able to help you decide what to use and what not to use, and help you determine your best ROI on technology.

What?

One of the biggest issues here is that most people haven't identified what success looks like—in other words, documenting what has to happen in order for you to be happy with your progress. For example: I want the first two pages of a Google search to refer to me exclusively; I want to increase my network to more than one thousand people; I want people to start calling me as the expert on environmental studies; I want others to comment on my blog posts 100 percent of the time; I want to increase my phone calls, sales results, and LinkedIn profile views by 10 percent. While the success of your newly implemented brand will not likely come all at once, you will notice the changes gradually. As long as you stay on top of your brand—asking yourself what steps you need to take to enhance your current brand, build your future brand, and break any negative brand items that exist—the changes will come.

Where?

Where will you invest your time, energy, and resources to get the maximum return? Also, where will you participate? There are hundreds of places where you can have a presence. The trick is to determine the ideal locations that will have the greatest impact for you. Your best bet on "where" is going to be determined by what you are trying to accomplish. If you are trying to manage your brand with your family, friends, and close acquaintances, then Facebook and Google+ could be good places to participate. If you are looking to manage your brand with employees, employers, or any other business contacts, then you would probably want to consider LinkedIn or a personal blog.

There really is no magic pill or right answer here. Just look to see where your target audiences participate the most online and go to that platform.

When?

Develop a proactive and systematic schedule for when you will write blog posts, update photos and videos, view comments, change banners, highlight brand items, and any other updates you can schedule. Consistency is the key. There are a bunch of very good studies that focus on when the best time of day and best days are to post items. The most diligent research and most compelling data come from the experts at HubSpot. They have published numerous studies, white papers, and stats that guide any person or company on what, when, and how to post. They have more than seven thousand companies with which they work, and the data that comes from this sample is extremely valuable.

One of the most simplistic yet beneficial segments in most of their research is the differentiation between personal and corporate, and business-to-business and business-to-consumer markets. (If you go to hubspot.com, you can view a lot of their awesome stats, reports, and resources.)

Every sector and region is slightly different; do some experimenting to find the right mix.

Why?

We covered this above, but to expand, this should be asked before you do anything online, corporately or personally. "Why am I posting or sending this?" You should be able to answer this question with an honest appraisal of its value. "Because I like it" is not enough in business; you need to have a genuine motive. If it doesn't provide value or get people thinking or talking, then why post it?

How?

Once you have thought through the questions above, you should be ready to develop a plan, no matter how simple or complex, for your digital marketing strategy.

Execution

Once you have your current and future brand clear in your mind, next you have to develop build-and-break plans. What are the items that you need to build your brand up, and what are the things that you need to stop?

- What will enhance your brand or move you to your future brand?

- What items will damage or deter your success?

- What are some "have-to" tactics that are nonnegotiable?

In this last part, it is crucial to be as detailed as possible. It also helps to document this process. For a practical guide and example of how to build a personal branding plan, as well as other resources, visit quintainmarketing.com/brandaid.

CHAPTER 4

Your Internet Footprint

(Be Careful Where You Step)

Personal branding is about managing your name—even if you don't own a business—in a world of misinformation, disinformation, and semi-permanent Google records. Going on a date? Chances are that your "blind" date has Googled your name. Going to a job interview? Ditto.

—Tim Ferriss, author of *The 4-Hour Workweek*

The Worldwide Backyard Barbecue

Before the Internet, it was a little easier to keep a low profile. It was also easier to manage your profile, through trusted friends, business contacts, and other direct, in-person communications. But that is no longer the case. Like it or not, the Internet has changed the way we communicate and perceive each other, and there's no turning back. Your online presence is as much a part of your brand as how you comport yourself in person—and arguably, it's the most important part. The Internet amplifies what we say and do, many times before people meet us in person. As in an echo chamber, what you say there doesn't stop when you close your mouth. It reverberates and has a life of its own, for better or worse. That's the danger of social media—and the opportunity.

Think of the Internet as a worldwide backyard barbecue. Everything you say and do online should be consistent with what you would say or do with your family, neighbors, colleagues, and friends—and anyone else you talk to face to face. And keep in mind that you can't see their faces now, so you can't react to feedback. Instead, you have to anticipate it.

. . . or a Cyber Country Club

In 2000, I was a member of two country clubs because a large number of my clients and prospects were members of those clubs. I wanted to hang out where my clients were hanging out. Today, I hang out on social media and in the cyber world. I could connect with three to five people per week at the country club. With big events a few times a year, I could get to see forty to fifty of them in a week. Today, I can reach hundreds of clients and prospects a day inside of my social media communities. There were numerous times in 2012 when I reached thousands with a single message.

You have the potential to develop a very large "cyber country club." Creating purposeful social media accounts, blogging, connecting with others who write blogs, commenting on others' articles and white papers, and being active in your social media will give you a group of people that can be your country club audience. It is not our purpose in this book to do specific social media training. There are very good specialists in this area who are keeping up with the daily changes and trends for social media maximization. Patrick does a great job of it, as well. A book can only present a snapshot of the best practices at the time it was written. One thing that *can* be taught in this book, though, is that creating a network of connections, and managing that network as a distribution system for whatever you want to sell or give to them, is critical if you want to maximize your potential for future success.

When I was in high school, one of my friends had a very wise father. He used to tell us, "If you are willing to see what you are doing or saying on the front page of the newspaper the next day, you can probably proceed with what you are doing. If you wouldn't want it on the front page of the newspaper, *stop* . . . immediately."

I had that thought on my mind throughout most of school, and it became even more important to me as I became a business executive who was building a reputation in the market.

This wise statement applies today in a much more complex way. The reality of any of our behaviors being on Facebook, Pinterest, YouTube, Google, a viral email, a viral text—the list goes on—is much greater than it was in the 1980s.

Avoiding brand damage online requires keeping a "front-page" mentality at the forefront of all your thoughts—and posts—at all times!

Here are some suggested processes that can help so you don't have to always remember:

- Ask yourself before posting on social media, "How will this impact my brand?"

- Have someone review your Internet presence on a weekly or monthly basis. My wife, my kids, my employees, Patrick, and my friends all know how important brand management is to me. They all look out for me and give me quick feedback, whether it's positive or negative, about what I show on the Internet. You can also pay someone who understands brand management to observe and give you regular feedback on your online presence. We use reputation.com to monitor our online presence. They manage the personal and corporate brands of some of the most powerful people in the world as well as many individuals who simply care about protecting their brand.

- Don't allow someone else to manage your brand online unless you have complete confidence in that person's understanding of your brand.

These three strategies are a good start. The best way to avoid brand damage, however, is to have a clear picture of what you want people to think of you, and maintain an attitude that everything you do will communicate this brand message to others.

"It's Facebook's Fault!"

I remember when Patrick told me he was leaving his college social media favorite for Facebook. I followed him to Facebook because he was the expert (and young and cool). He has done a great job of helping me use Facebook as a powerful and relevant part of my brand management. He has given the following advice to me and our clients.

Facebook plays a complex, and continually evolving, role in our lives. Some people spend many hours a day on the site. Others rarely visit it, or avoid it altogether due to concerns over privacy, overheated political arguments with acquaintances from grade school, or too many requests for a game of pretend farming or jewel crushing. Some blame Facebook for their own gaffes and misjudgments. It's become all too

> In the end, it's up to each of us to be our own brand manager on Facebook, just as we are everywhere else.

easy to make Facebook itself a scapegoat for our own missteps online. Sure, its privacy settings are overly complicated and change all the time—but in the end, it's up to each of us to be our own brand manager on Facebook, just as we are everywhere else.

If you're tempted to discount Facebook as merely a personal space, wholly separate from professional life, and a non-business space, we would advise you to reconsider. First, and perhaps most obvious, there is always crossover between our personal and professional selves. Most of us have Facebook friends who are our colleagues, direct reports, bosses, or industry peers "in real life." It's a fact worth remembering when you post photos, late-night status updates, and even items that reflect your political views or religious beliefs.

In addition, Facebook has become a professional space in its own right. Many people—Patrick and I included—use Facebook pages as part of their business. More than half of our clients and many of our prospects are connected to us on Facebook. The depth of relationships with these people is incredible. It helps our ability to serve these clients when we know them more intimately through Facebook. We know it exposes our lives and theirs. But it also deepens the relationship, and our businesses are positively impacted by this intimacy. Also, we have been purposefully looking at the frequency in which people recommend products, post negatively about products, refer to businesses in posts, and ask for recommendations on Facebook. About half of the posts on our Facebook home page mention a company or a product. Social media is the word of mouth of today. The word of mouth that comes through a "personal" site is frequent and powerful. I bet the initial sales of this book will be more influenced through Facebook than any other social media. I encourage you to think deeply about how all forms of social media may play a role in your personal and business brand strategy.

Google It!

Patrick's firm, Quintain Marketing, is a leader in global digital marketing. It helps clients increase their web traffic, convert that traffic into leads, and eventually turn those leads into clients. They help them grow their business by enhancing their web presence.

One of Quintain Marketing's areas of expertise is search engine optimization (SEO). The value of SEO, as Patrick sees it, is twofold. First, it can help ensure that all of the results on the first page from a search on a person or company are positive. Second, it can help companies identify what search terms they want to be found for so they turn up in Internet search results even when potential customers are searching an industry or service, not for them specifically.

Just as Quintain Marketing uses SEO with clients, they also do it for themselves. If you do an online search for "Quintain Marketing," you will find the first page of results to all be positive and relevant. This is because it is so good at managing what Google and other search engines reveal about the company.

Just as potential customers search for our clients, and us, people are searching for you as well. With Google and other search engines directing people to the most relevant information

> It is now almost as important to consider what Google "thinks" about you as what people think about you.

on the web, it is now almost as important to consider what Google "thinks" about you as what people think about you.

Search Engine Optimization 101

Again, this is another area of Patrick's expertise. SEO is a valuable brand management technique. Below are some strategies Patrick uses to manage his clients' SEO.

To begin, do a vanity search by typing your name into your search engine of choice. Go ahead, I'll wait. . . .

Ta-da! That's your personal brand. To those who don't know you intimately, that is the information that tells them who you are. Did the result come back with positive information? Was it relevant? Was it even you? Whether you are a recent grad looking for an internship or a seasoned professional, the first-page results of a web search define you. As mentioned before, there is plenty of evidence to suggest that people are looking you up prior to meeting face-to-face, and what they find determines what they think of you. Your reputation (brand) certainly precedes you.

Everything you post (your digital footprint) and everything that people post about you (your digital shadow) shapes your brand online. Erik Qualman, bestselling author of *Socialnomics* and *Digital Leader*, defines this as your "digital stamp." (Do a quick Google search of "Erik Qualman" and "digital stamp" to see the power of this concept.) With all of the available information on you, only the top seven to ten results really matter. That's right—only the first seven to ten. There are a lot of varying statistics out there, but a common one states that less than 6 percent of people go to the second page and beyond on Google. This means that 94 percent of people searching for information on you will shape their opinion by first-page results only! The good news is that you can take steps to manage what this all-important yet "byte-size" picture says about you, and in turn manage your digital stamp.

> With all of the available information on you, only the top seven to ten results really matter.

Just as many corporations use SEO tactics, you can do the same for yourself. As Patrick and his team at Quintain Marketing describe it, SEO is a method for getting your website, content, or brand to rank higher in search engines (e.g., Google, Yahoo!, and Bing) so that it appears first—or at least on the first page—when people search for your type of product, service, or area of expertise.

A traditional SEO campaign compares your goals with the online search results for your website. Changes can be made to your site itself while trying to increase your organic rankings through links placed throughout the website. SEO helps the search engines recognize your relevance to specific keywords that people search for online. The search engine optimization process includes researching keywords, creating content, building links, and making sure your website and online profiles are as visible as possible within these search engines.

The first step of SEO campaigns is to define the words and phrases necessary to attract relevant visitors to your site. These keywords should be words that best describe your company and the page you are trying to promote.

Below are a few of Patrick's tips to manage your personal brand online through SEO.

Keywords

Start by generally defining what value you provide and what you do. Write down the general words that you would want to be found for online. Yes, your name and all of its variations should be included in your list. But what are the key attributes you want to be known for? What keywords and search terms best describe how you want to be seen? Be sure to include them, along with variations thereof. A few examples are adviser, brand expert, personal branding, or speaker. Be as specific as possible.

Long-Tail Keywords

Long-tail is a term that means less common and more descriptive and/or including an extended definition. Once you've determined your general list, you need to manipulate the words to get very specific. For example, it would be almost impossible (and extremely expensive) to be found using general words like *digital marketing, insurance,* or *financial planner.* These words are highly searched and therefore competitive to rank for and expensive to do any kind of pay-per-click or Google AdWords campaign. Creating more specific keyword phrases like *small business digital marketing consultant, insurance adviser to nonprofits,* or *certified financial planner, Richmond, Virginia,* however, are going to be easier to rank.

Get Social

Major social networks like LinkedIn, Google+, Facebook, Twitter, YouTube, Vimeo, etc., tend to rank very high in search results. The more you are on these sites, the more chances you have to show up on the first page of search results. Post photos from events, presentations, status updates that reinforce your desired image and message, positive reviews of your recent performance, and so on. But remember: optimization only helps you if you do it thoughtfully. All too often negative exposure is the unintended consequence. If you don't want to be found in a search for "drunken holiday party karaoke," well, you know what *not* to post.

Be careful here. Don't join every social network out there and then abandon or neglect your various profiles. You have to proactively manage them, stay active, and be social. A neglected profile could do you more damage than good (you risk seeming out of date, out of touch, and inactive in every sense of the word).

Customize Your Public Profile URL on All Social Networks

Most social networks allow you to customize the URL for your profile page. Don't get too creative here. Google won't know it's you if you use a URL such as /crazygurl420. Use your name—and if your name is taken, use a variation on it (Bob instead of Robert, Susan instead of Sue, try your middle initial, add your city, and so on). But keep it simple and transparent. The goal is to be easily found.

Google+

You might think Google+ is only for group chats, or perhaps you've never heard much about it at all, preferring to use Facebook or Twitter as your social media site of choice. But think about it: Google has a vested interest in including its own social media site, and weighting it heavily, in their search results. Like it or not, your Google+ profile is essential for this reason—and a great tool for managing your personal brand.

Make sure you set up a Google+ account and fill out your profile completely and thoughtfully, using your desired keywords and search terms.

> Like it or not, your Google+ profile is essential.

Content

In order to create more and more information about you and your expertise, you will need to create content. Yes, this means writing. Blogging, guest blogging, writing articles and white papers are all opportunities to demonstrate your expertise. Your writing should be focused on your list of keywords. Make sure the title and copy of your content include a few of your keywords as well.

SEO Packages

If you have your own site, there are plenty of SEO plug-ins (especially on WordPress) that do the hand-holding for you. Also, other content management systems like HubSpot come packed full of great modules that help you manage keywords and SEO.

There is great opportunity in managing what people see when they are searching for you. It does take some work, but following the steps above will help you bring relevant, positive information to the forefront of search results.

We're All Stalkers Now (Sort Of)

Patrick and I always try to learn as much about someone as we can early on in a relationship. And why shouldn't we? The information is readily available.

Recently, Patrick had an initial call with a potential client in Iowa. The conversation went fine and was very typical. There were a few quick pleasantries, such as "Tell me about your company," "What are you trying to get accomplished?" and so on. Nothing fantastic. Immediately after the call, Patrick pulled up a few social sites and requested to connect with the potential client. Within a few hours they were "friends" on several sites.

After fifteen minutes of research, Patrick knew that the man was a Notre Dame graduate and a raving fan of the Fighting Irish sports program. He learned that the man was married with two young kids. Through recent posts he discovered the man had just returned from a trip to the Dominican Republic and had stayed at the resort that was featured on one of Patrick's favorite outdoors shows. He knew more about this person than he could have gleaned from several phone conversations. He also got to view pictures taken from his agency's offices, and got a chance to get a feel for their work environment.

The next call went much differently. Patrick was able to discuss college football, the Dominican Republic, aspects of their shared office culture, and even that travel TV show. There was much more of a connection than in the first phone call. No, knowing where the man had gone to school and where he spent his vacation did not automatically convince him to become a client. What it did do, though, was break down the barriers and allow them to speak as individuals, not faceless business drones on the either end of a phone.

Patrick told this story at a recent sales leadership workshop in Boston, and his new "friend" Chris was in the audience. Patrick was very open about the research that he had done and how it affected their relationship initially. At the end of the story, Chris blurted out, "Man, you were kind of stalking me online . . . but it definitely worked."

MAKING THE MOST OF LINKEDIN

I have watched LinkedIn grow over the past eight years. In the beginning, it looked like a place for salespeople to market to each other. I felt like I needed to be there, but wasn't too worried about anyone finding me on it except someone trying to sell me something. Since those early days, my view has changed dramatically. The site has become very robust, with a staggering increase in the number of users (according to *Fortune* magazine, an eye-opening 141 million unique visitors were on LinkedIn in April 2013 alone). These users spent an average of twenty minutes per session—longer than on many other websites. That is a serious brand communication opportunity.

Today, I manage my presence on LinkedIn carefully, and I consider it a primary tool for my brand management. I receive more than two hundred visitors to my page each month, and my profile appears in more than 1,800 LinkedIn searches monthly. That's a lot of brand impressions, built and maintained over time.

The keyword is *maintained*. Whether you want them to or not, people—colleagues, potential employers, prospective new clients, and others—are looking you up on LinkedIn, and often forming a first impression of you there. As with all opportunities to shape our brand, we can take an active role, or we can let others come to their own conclusions without our input. The former is a far better strategy.

Patrick has developed a powerful LinkedIn management tool that provides insights into proactive use of LinkedIn for prospecting, personal profile management, data management, SEO, managing endorsements and referrals, and much more. If you want to maximize your efforts on LinkedIn, it would be best to take a class, call a consultant, or contact Quintain Marketing for this resource. I am going to pull some of the information from this resource, however, and combine with my expertise on brand management to give you my top ten critical ways to manage your brand on LinkedIn:

1. Make sure to have a good-quality, professional picture on your profile. This may be the first time someone sees you. Give a great first impression. Like it or not, in many cases people make decisions on relationships based on how you look. Have a welcoming smile, sharp dress, and look like the brand you want to portray.

2. Write a strong Summary statement. People are typically not going to read everything in your profile. One of the first things they will see is your Summary statement. Make sure to express your brand as clearly as possible in this section.

3. Make sure to have someone review your profile for spelling and grammar. You will certainly have a brand problem if someone sees errors throughout your profile.

4. Have your recommendations reflect what you want people to think about you. If the recommendations are positive but reflect commoditized, oversimplified, or outdated attributes, it could conflict with what you want people to

continued on next page . . .

think. For example, an insurance salesperson who wants to be known for helping with strategies beyond insurance should be sure his recommendations don't all simply reflect that he's "a great insurance agent."

5. Stay active on your page. Post information a minimum of two times a week. (Don't post *too* often or you will get a brand of being on social media all the time.) Staying active will keep your brand fresh in your connections' minds.

6. Make sure your profile is 100 percent complete and follow the steps in the Profile Strength suggestions. Customize your URL. Try to choose a URL that matches your full name. This helps with search engine optimization.

7. Make sure all information is correct and updated regularly. Make sure to turn off the "activity broadcast" if you are going to make a lot of changes, however. You don't want to flood your connections with updates.

8. Make sure to add your brand items into the endorsements section. Then encourage your connections to endorse you in those areas.

9. Incorporate your personality beyond work. Highlight philanthropic work, social organizations, and personal interests that will enhance and support your brand. You want readers to genuinely like you and want to know you after viewing your profile. Most profiles look like a résumé and are not inviting on a personal level.

10. Keep your recommendations fresh. Recommendations that are all a few years old will cause questions to be asked about your current value.

LinkedIn is not the end-all of managing your brand. But it has become such a popular resource that you can almost guarantee you will have weekly visitors. This is a very easy and powerful way to let people know what they should think about you.

Other Technology

Another very good site is 123people.com. This site pulls all of the information on you from the Internet and organizes it in a way so that you can clearly see what you are telling people to think of you. All you have to do is type in your name, and within milliseconds your entire brand is displayed on one web page. At first, you may be overwhelmed and terrified at the detailed and accurate information that is displayed. Next, a sense of panic may occur when you see the type of information that is included. Your digital footprint shows images, videos, articles on or about you, recommendations, bios, products that you have developed or are associated with, your connections, your likes and dislikes, education, local involvement, tax records, [gulp] criminal records, your thoughts and conversations (blog), marriage and/or divorce records, social profiles, past jobs, and expertise. All of this is displayed elegantly on one page.

Probably the best function on the site is the tag cloud. This widget pulls the top keywords associated with your name. After you have looked through all of the painstaking details about yourself, you are now presented with an even more rudimentary list at the bottom of the page. Talk about a swift kick to the stomach.

The silver lining in all of this is that this information can be managed. If you are proactively managing your brand, playing good offense and defense, managing keywords, and optimizing technology, then this site should excite you. It will give you instant gratification, knowing that you are doing a great job managing your brand. On the other hand, it may be the wake-up call you've needed. You may run this report on yourself and be displeased with the results. Even worse, you could do the search and realize that the information that comes back is for someone else with the same name as you.

Patrick and his team at Quintain Marketing have used this site with many of their clients and have run hundreds of tests. They have searched celebrities as well as ordinary citizens, and everyone in between. The two detrimental outcomes of poor information or misinformation are common. As an example, we ran an insurance agency CEO through the system. None—not a single item—of the information that came back was about him. We were hoping that some very clear, powerful words and information would show up. We were hoping that he was closely tied to his organization and vice versa. This was not the case. The images were of other people, tricycles, and other irrelevant objects. There were no correct contact options, and his tag cloud looked like it should be associated with a local tattoo parlor rather than a major corporation. There were words like *tattoo*, *tattoo shop*, *photography*, *foods*, and other places and things that certainly do not describe him. What if a large prospect or insurance company connection searched him? What would they think about this CEO?

You may be thinking, Well, maybe he has a very common name, or, He is secretly a tattoo enthusiast. First, I can promise you that he does not and is not. Second, so what if he did have a common name? Should he just give up and assume that there is nothing he can do to fix this? Absolutely not. There are several ways to make the results for your name and your brand not only about you but also positive.

Try the site out for yourself. What if your name is John Smith or Jane Doe? Does that mean that you should just chalk up a bad Internet footprint to that fact? Or does it make sense to do everything in your power to make sure that you are the one who is attached to that name? To make sure that the information and media presented are about you?

"So Much Cooler Online"

A few years ago, I got a call from Patrick, who said, "You have to hear this song." He put on Brad Paisley's country tune called "Online." In the song, Paisley describes a lovable loser who is a social outcast. But as the song progresses, he sings,

Online I live in Malibu, I pose for Calvin Klein,
I've been in GQ, I'm single and I'm rich,
And I've got a set of six-pack abs that would blow your mind.

He continues on with a lot of statements about who he "is" when he's hiding behind the safety of a computer screen.

Patrick went on to explain that the takeaway from this song shouldn't be to lie about your stats or be deceitful online. You have to be genuine in your message and brand no matter how you are communicating it. If you manufacture a false identity or brand, you will eventually be discovered. A client may find out that you are not as experienced as you said you are, an employer will find out that you aren't "as advertised," and, like the song above, a potential date will soon find out that your six-pack abs more closely resemble a keg.

The song does, however, portray a very valuable (and, yes, comical) message about the power of online branding. If you manage your brand through different social media, websites, and other media, then you can, in fact, quickly manage your future brand. Again, we aren't suggesting that you portray a false image or information. What we are suggesting is that there is real power in speed and communicating your message through technology.

> There is real power in speed and communicating your message through technology.

Six Pixels

In grade school, you probably heard about Frigyes Karinthy or at least his theory of six degrees of separation, which he developed in 1912. His famous theory, later studied by psychologist Stanley Milgram, stated that everyone on Earth could be connected to any other person by a chain of no more than five acquaintances. Now, let's fast-forward a hundred years or so and introduce advanced technology to the equation. The Internet and social media applications have now shrunk the six degrees dramatically. We fully believe that you are no more than one or two connections away from anyone on the planet. Mitch Joel described this in his book *Six Pixels of Separation*. The subtitle—"Everyone Is Connected. Connect Your Business to Everyone."—suggests that it is crucial for individuals and organizations to maximize their presence and optimize technology to work in their favor.

This idea of six pixels separating us all can be wildly optimistic, or it can also be devastatingly damaging. To echo earlier statements, if you believe that you are or could be proactively managing your brand online, then you

> You are no more than one or two connections away from anyone on the planet.

will most likely see the six pixels as a great opportunity. If you are not managing your brand or Internet footprint, then you could be in serious trouble.

If you are truly one or two pixels or connections away from anyone, what does that mean? What if you could connect to the prospect you've been trying to meet, a decision maker at your dream job, an alumni who can get you into your school of choice, or someone famous? Oh, the possibilities! But if you can find them, then they can just as easily find you. What would happen if they did search for you? Would they find the person you truly are? Or would they find a damaging online version and a perception that screams *run*?

Managing your Internet footprint is certainly not the only way to manage your brand, but if you ignore it, your brand could quickly come crashing down.

Seven Types of Profiles

Matt Morehead is the CEO of Launch2Life, a program to help twentysomethings get started in careers by understanding basic principles of finance, budgeting, insurance, networking, etc. He shared with us a humorous and insightful list of the most common types of profiles he sees clients posting online.

Tireless Self-Promoter

These individuals are constantly telling people about themselves. They often annoyingly promote their company, product, services, and philanthropic ventures. Instead of balancing personal and professional information, they tend to go overboard with their promotions. These people usually get hidden or removed as a connection altogether.

Never-Ending Christmas Letter

Before technology made it extremely easy for us to let people into our lives, we had to find other ways to let people know how we were and what we were up to. Remember the annual five-page letter in the envelope with the Christmas card? These letters were basically a year in review of the family sending the card. They typically give us great messages about how fabulous everyone is doing. Little Suzy has been accepted into Mensa, Johnny is the best player on his team, and the father of the family got a huge promotion at work. You rarely hear about the bad or mediocre stuff that happened during the year. These "everything is rosy" type of postings make you wonder about who they really are and what is really going on behind the scenes.

Those in this group are constantly promoting how great their lives are. Every day they are blessed because something amazing and wonderful happened. If you are like me, you know that bad stuff is also happening to them—that's life. These people seem fake and exaggerated.

Self-Appointed Motivator

These people belong to the quote-of-the-day crowd. These people have taken the charge of motivating their entire friend circle online.

They post quotes, spiritual sayings, and motivations to get through the workweek—welcome or not.

Attention Seeker

This is the FML crowd. (If you don't know what FML stands for, you'll have to Google it.) These individuals dramatize everything that happens to them. I once saw a girl post, "The window in my new BMW 328i is stuck, so I am sitting in the service center getting it fixed—FML." Sure, car trouble is bothersome, but FML? Really? Ninety-eight percent of the world would love to have that problem.

The Flame Thrower

This group is comprised of divisively opinionated people. They take every chance to comment and argue about politics, religion, sports, and so on. These people tend to take things very seriously and can easily offend others—in fact, that often seems to be the goal.

The Voyeur

Those in this group are out there, but they don't share anything. They either don't check their account very often, or they sit back and watch all the activity without contributing anything of their own. This is a dangerous group to be in. We typically tell people to delete their account if that is their approach. It is more damaging to have an outdated or blank account than to not participate online at all. These onlookers aren't using social

> It is more damaging to have an outdated or blank account than to not participate online at all.

media in the way that it is intended to be used—for being social. You have to have a balance of give and take to be seen as an authority or relevant in the social media space.

Observer/Commenter

This is the group that gets it!

These people find ways to start and enter conversations. They comment on current events, repost useful information, balance the professional with the personal, and are always conscious of their personal brand. They understand how their interactions online can affect their brand, and they make decisions based on that understanding.

They use social media to foster and maintain personal and professional relationships, establish their expertise and authority in the areas that they want to, and as a bonus oftentimes pick up new clients because of their efforts.

So which one are you?

Can you name a person to whom you are connected in each group? Does that support or damage their brand or yours?

No News Is Bad News

I spoke at a large business executive conference about personal branding. During the speech I asked how often people felt they were looked up on the Internet both professionally and personally. With a request for showing hands at different frequencies, some raised their hands at one to five times per month, a few more at six to ten times per month, and most felt like they were looked up at least eleven to twenty times a month.

I also asked the participants to raise their hand if they thought it would increase over time. One hundred percent of the people in the room raised their hand, agreeing that more and more people will be researching personal and professional relationships on the Internet prior to first meetings.

When the speech ended, a gentleman in his mid-fifties came directly to the stage to meet me. I had been aware of this man during the speech because he had a look of doubt and resistance regarding the message. I expected that the man was not going to praise the brilliance of my speech. I assumed he would inform me of his experience and why I was wrong. He didn't disappoint!

The gentleman was very well dressed and gave a look of confidence as he began to speak. "Mr. Linne, I would like to introduce myself" (I won't use his name). "I completely agree with the comments and points you made in your speech. When you were talking about how often people will look us up online, however, I thought of something you haven't thought about!"

His bait intrigued me. I asked him to enlighten me.

He said, "I laughed when you were speaking, because I thought 'If someone looks me up online, he won't find anything!' I guess my brand is pretty safe. I don't do any social media, online pictures or videos, no web page, nothing." His chest was out a bit now. "So what do you think of that?"

I was in a hurry to leave the event, so I decided to respond to this gentleman in a way that would make my point quickly but leave him speechless.

"Sir, I am impressed," I began. "I have a game I like to play with individuals in my audiences. Would you mind if I played it with you?"

He showed a bit of fear in his face but responded positively. "Okay, sure."

I continued, "I would like to take a shot at defining your brand."

He stood up tall and had that salesman-like, know-it-all smirk. He said, "Take your best shot."

"Okay, here it goes. You are a salesman near the end of your career. You used to be successful but have not experienced the same level of success you enjoyed early in your career. You are not technology savvy and would not be able to react to or be proactive in working with a client if technology were required. You are seen and known as 'old school' and would struggle in selling to a modern buyer. You are a nice guy, but a large number of people probably feel sorry for you that you have stopped learning and growing." I paused. Then I asked, "How'd I do?"

He looked at me, stunned, and with a frown said, "You're probably right."

I responded, "So if others look you up on the Internet and can't find you, it helps to identify your brand."

"Touché!" he said as he simulated a knife going into his gut. "I guess you got me there. I better get busy on my brand."

He gave me a handgun shot and a wink. Again, his brand was defined even more as he walked away.

You may not want to be found on the Internet. That is okay, as long as you are okay with how that impacts your brand.

CHAPTER 5

The Best Offense Is a Good Defense

Protecting Your Brand

It takes twenty years to build a reputation and five minutes to ruin it. If you think about that, you'll do things differently.

—Warren Buffett

Age of the Big Offense

The NFL has had major changes in the last ten years. The New England Patriots, Denver Broncos, Green Bay Packers, San Francisco 49ers, and Washington Redskins were all big offense teams that made it to the playoffs. Big offenses have taken over the game and are dominating in on-field and off-field performance (i.e., money). It is the age of the big offense. They said that the offense wins games but defense wins Super Bowls. That was true for more than forty years, but the past six Super Bowls have proven the power of a big offense.

As an ex-NFL offensive player, I see an offense as something that is taking initiative and pushing toward results. A great offense can make changes based on the conditions that change around it. The key is to find the competitive advantage and exploit it. This new NFL style is risky, aggressive, and bold, and it uses multiple resources and stays ahead of the competition (and most defenses).

For example, when Tim Tebow stepped into the Broncos' starting offense in 2011, he had a great run for six games and startled the world with a "different" offense. By the time he played the New England Patriots, he was considered a potential Pro Bowl candidate. Unfortunately for him (and Bronco fans), Tim ran into a coach who had figured out that offensive scheme and destroyed it. Then every team after that figured him out and shut him down. Game over. The need for reinvention had to begin.

The same thing is happening with personal brand management. What I am doing today to manage my brand with blogs, video blogs, videos, Twitter, Facebook, LinkedIn, voice and screen capture software, voice mail, and public appearances could be worthless and dead a year from now. Continued change to the conditions around us is critical to a successful brand. We have to be aggressive with what is available to communicate our brand. We also have to be aware of trends and buyer behaviors to not get left behind.

I hesitate to spell out the details of how to execute an offensive strategy. Things are changing very fast. Whatever I communicate that needs to be done today will probably be obsolete in a few months. So keep in mind the concepts more than the details of the strategy.

My Current Offensive Strategy

- Perform quarterly review of what I want people to think of me. I have mentioned numerous times that your brand is what people think of you. A desired brand is what you want people to think of you. I find it critical to visit my brand every ninety days. This is because things change fast and new habits can form. Determining what I desire others to think of me is the first step to getting them to think it. This quarterly exercise gives me new clarity and helps me keep it top of mind.

- Solicit annual feedback from friends, business associates, and family on what they think about me (my brand). My friends and coworkers have learned how powerful proactive brand management can be, so we frequently give each other feedback on our brands. I ask people throughout my workplace what they think and what they believe my brand is to others. It is a great exercise, because I learn a lot. The best advice I can give you here is to always say thank you for advice. Never question it, challenge it, or disagree with it. If you do, you will never get honest feedback again. Just say thank you, and deal with it as a perception (positive or negative).

- Review what I wear, what I drive, and how I act. These items impact my brand, and therefore I am purposeful about each of them. I actually dress way down locally because I don't do business in my town. Therefore, I want my personal brand to be different from my business brand.

- Use video blogs on the front of a personal website and a company website. Keeping active in as many places as possible gives me a broader reach with my brand. Frequent video updates on my sites keep people coming back to watch what I have to say. It also helps get my name at the top of the list in a Google search.

- Maintain written blogs on the front of a personal website and a company website. Keeping fresh and making sure my blog messages support my brand is necessary and valuable. My wife has a couple of blogs, and people love reading her work. You don't have to be a published author to have something to say and share with others. Learn to blog, have fun giving others ideas and thoughts, and package them in ways to create interest and challenge. It will give you a great brand.

- Write guest blog posts for other influential websites. I write blogs for a few different organizations. People are looking for content. If you can write something with fresh content, reach out and offer to write something for an organization that can help your brand.

- Keep an active Twitter account to push articles, thoughts, intellectual capital, and brand messages. This is the key strategy to expand my network. Twitter allows you to push articles and ideas to your network. If the content is high quality, your connections will retweet those messages. When new people see quality content, they will connect with you. This is the method that allows you to expand your network quickly. I had fewer than a hundred friends on LinkedIn for six years. I had more than one thousand friends in six months when I used my Twitter and LinkedIn combination push strategy.

- Create a LinkedIn page to be found by business relationships. It is also an offensive strategy to see who is looking me up, and to reach out to first- and second-level relationships. This is by far the most powerful and effective way to expand your professional reach. After all, that is why LinkedIn was created in the first place.

- Use a personal Facebook account to push my "human" brand. As an author, speaker, and industry thought leader, I am at times seen as untouchable. I connect with people on Facebook to show that I have a family and do normal things like bike ride, work out, etc. Some people say, "I don't want to share my personal information out there on Facebook. I don't think other people care what I am doing." I find it interesting that those people will tell all the folks at their country club that information. You have to put it in perspective. I believe it is valuable to share your personal side with people. We can connect on a much deeper level with people if they know us as a father, husband, friend, coach, etc. Facebook allows us to be real people and share that with others. I love how I can connect with more than half of my clients on the personal side of their lives through Facebook. Knowing we have kids, spouses, and life challenges can bring great value to our relationships. We can be misunderstood a lot in our lives, but Facebook helps people see the deeper purpose of my life, and it provides others with a clear picture of why I do all the things I do in my life.

- Maintain a business Facebook page for communicating updates to my products and latest business ideas. This page is the least active of all my offensive strategies, though I consider it critical because it is another measure of success (based on the number of "likes" the page receives). Facebook creates the opportunity for buzz and talk about my businesses. It is another world of connectivity. Creating connected groups that are interested in my work has great benefit. People frequently comment to me about my posts and thought leadership. I make sure to post thoughts and comments on the site on a regular basis—though not too often or people will think I don't have anything else to do but post on my Facebook page (that would be a negative brand). Good-quality content that makes people think or inspires them is what I want on my company Facebook page.

- Attend key industry and business events as a speaker. This strategy allows me to tell people what to think of me. I get frequent requests to speak at events all over the world. Not everyone will get these kinds of opportunities. If you can learn to become an engaging speaker, however, the opportunities are endless. Local clubs, schools, businesses, and all kinds of events are looking for emcees, speakers, teachers, and those who can present and entertain. This could be a good strategy to include in one's brand.

Managing your brand by waiting for others to figure it out will guarantee you have a brand you don't want. Be aggressive, and find the media outlets that will get your brand in front of the right people. You may make some mistakes in this strategy. Even Tom Brady has thrown interceptions. But he comes back and throws a few touchdown passes, and the interception is forgotten. If you are aggressive with your brand, you can overcome a lot of mistakes with the right media at the right time.

Just keep in mind what we taught earlier in the book. Before you do anything, make sure to ask yourself, how will this activity impact how others think of me?

A Defense Can Lose the Game

The excitement from sporting events comes from action: the walk-off home runs, eighty-yard touchdown runs, buzzer-beating three-pointers, and penalty kicks. Most spectators don't go to watch a shutout from the home team pitcher, a great performance from the defensive line, or a brilliantly executed flat-back four in soccer. The glory is almost always in the offense. Most sports have proven in the past few years that offense will clearly win games; defenses, however, have proven they can lose games as well. The same goes for personal branding.

Protecting your brand through defensive strategies may be just as important as having good offensive strategies. You can have a fantastic set of differentiating brand items, a top-notch communication strategy, and the most positive reputation around. But without a defensive process to complement this, your offense could fizzle. One negative interaction, one instant, or one misstep can damage everything.

Jenga

Patrick and I were talking about personal branding and thinking of ways to help our clients manage their brands more successfully. He told me to imagine a Jenga game with all the blocks stacked high. Then he proceeded to tell me how brand management was like a game of Jenga. If you have ever played this game, then you know how fragile this stack of blocks can be. Every block is stacked carefully, crisscrossed and all interdependent. In case you haven't played, the objective is to take turns removing one block at a time. You can remove any block you like, from any level. As the game goes on, the stack becomes more and more unstable. Most times it takes several moves or removals of blocks to finally get the stack to crumble. At any point, one mistake, one error, or one miscalculation can send the entire stack crashing down. If your move knocks over the stack, then you lose.

Now imagine that this represents your branding strategy. Every individual block represents a different strategy or tactic. They represent the hours spent on determining your future brand, the media in place to support it, your Internet footprint that you've worked so hard to manage, and your reputation in your marketplace or circle of influence. As with the real game, one false move could cause you to lose, causing your whole strategy to crumble.

What's worse is that other people are trying to sabotage your game as well. So not only do you need to be extremely careful in managing your own strategy, you also need to constantly be aware of what others are doing. If you don't monitor your game (branding strategy), someone can come in and ruin it. She could post damaging content about you, trash you in a blog post or tweet, or take a statement you make the wrong way. Fortunately, in brand management you have the ability to bury bad posts and manage your SEO to get the right information to the top. Unlike the permanent nature of each Jenga game, you have the ability to change the game with personal branding and reset the board. But the key is to be on top of the monitoring. Without your realizing it, the market may be getting a very incorrect message about you, causing damage to your reputation. Some basic strategies can include having a third-party review all your media prior to placing it in public, getting a proofreader, outsourcing your writing, having a PR or digital marketing company on retainer in case of a major negative event, frequently doing searches on yourself to see what others are saying/posting about you, and ultimately asking yourself that important question before doing or communicating anything in public media: How will this impact what others think of me? (We will address a more specific defensive strategy later in this chapter.)

One Block Out of Place

Years ago, casino mogul Stephen Wynn made an interesting comment during a keynote speech at a Charles Schwab conference. He said that it only takes one poor client experience to ruin an entire company. This seems like a huge claim coming from a man who owns several of the top casinos on the Vegas Strip. He has thousands of customers pour through his doors every day. How could he possibly think that just one poor experience could ruin his entire organization? Simple. It's the same principle as Jenga. One damaging experience at the wrong time and wrong place could have a rippling (and crippling) effect on your brand, leaving it almost irreparable.

Birds of a Feather

I referred to this earlier. Often overlooked in branding are the people, groups, organizations, and events to which you are connected. Who and what you choose to connect with says a lot about who you are. These connections can either enhance people's perception of you, or they can severely damage your brand. As they say, birds of a feather flock together.

One of Patrick's friends told him an amazing story about the power of connections. His former roommate from school connected with him on Facebook. He hadn't talked to the guy since they were in school together but thought it would be good to see what he was up to. Very shortly after connecting with him, his old roommate went through his entire friend list and connected with all of the attractive women on his list, including his fiancée. These women saw the requests and thought it was one of his buddy's good friends, so most accepted the request.

It became very clear that this guy had a lifestyle that didn't match up with my friend's brand. He was connecting with bondage and porn sites, and he was responding to events such as an S&M conference in Vegas. Patrick's friend was horrified to see these online behaviors. The fact that many of his female friends saw these behaviors became quite a challenge for him. They began to ask him about this guy and wondered why they were friends. Patrick's buddy had to play defense and explain that they were roommates in school and not true friends. This activity made people question his friend (though it didn't have any lasting effects, as he is very good at managing his own brand), so he deleted his old roommate as an online friend. He didn't want to be associated with this kind of behavior or lifestyle. Even though he wasn't the one doing these things, it still trickled to him based on his connection with his old roommate.

Your connections can either enhance what you are trying to portray, or they can hurt you.

Defensive Game Plan

So what are some ways to play defense? In a lot of ways, the steps to a great defense are similar to the steps for a great offense. Look for potential problems before they become a reality—if you see a place where your defenses are weak, it's time to sharpen them up.

Do an Analysis

As mentioned earlier, words, actions, thoughts, appearance, interactions, etc., either support or damage your brand. A good exercise is to determine what items support or enhance your brand and what items damage it. To do this, simply split a sheet of paper into two columns. Label the columns "What enhances my brand" and "What damages my brand." Think about voice tonality, posture, posts you make, information you share with others, your peer group, how you behave at work, and what is communicated about you outside of work. Place those current items in the appropriate columns.

Next, develop build-and-break plans. What should you do on a regular basis to maintain your brand? What more could you be doing? And what should you avoid or stop? Create a list of action items.

Regular Audits

Just like in Jenga, you have to be in control of your moves. You cannot allow others to ruin your strategy for you. You have to be the one in control. Items to constantly be aware of are what is being said and what information can be linked to you. If you are aware of what information the marketplace is receiving about you, then you can react quickly and make adjustments or support the information.

Technology can certainly help you here. Try setting up alerts on your name, company, competitors, and organizations that you are involved with. See what is being said about you, both good and bad. If you are playing good defense, then you will always be several steps ahead. Careful monitoring of items such as pictures, videos, articles, and comments is crucial.

Another real risk is someone hacking your accounts and spamming your contacts or sending viruses or damaging content. You need to minimize your risk of being hacked. This is accomplished by changing your passwords frequently, having complex passwords, not opening unfamiliar emails, and using up-to-date security protection systems. You certainly don't want someone going out there and representing you negatively. Remember, information moves fast.

Outsource

It is becoming very affordable to have someone manage and monitor your brand. The return on investment can be well worth it. Having someone spend time weekly on your brand to check the market and monitor information could pay for itself by avoiding one negative event.

If you aren't monitoring your brand and media, it could have a lasting damaging impact.

Recently, Patrick had a conversation with Michael Fertik, the founder of Reputation.com, about online reputation management. They discussed the monumental shift that has happened with our reputation, brand, and privacy. Michael explained that without ever announcing it, the Internet has taken control of our reputation. That is a scary idea. People can post anything they like about you, true or not. Additionally, your private information can be shared freely, and you are supposed to just deal with it because that is the "new normal."

The sad truth is that people and organizations tend to see personal branding and reputation management as either not important or far too big of a task to take on. Instead of learning about ways to truly manage their information and reputation, they make a few low-level changes with the hope that it will solve all of their problems. Michael said, "People change a few privacy settings in Facebook and think they've done their job. The 'bunker mentality' is not online reputation management."

When Patrick asked Michael why he started Reputation.com, he expected to hear a backstory of how his brand had been damaged, leading to professional harm. That was not the case. Instead, Michael said, "I saw the way that we were losing control of ourselves and our dignity. I only saw this problem getting bigger, not smaller."

CHAPTER 6

Repairing Brand Damage

My reputation grows with every failure.
—George Bernard Shaw

In Chapter 1, I told the story of a board member at a construction firm who, after earning the respect of his peers at a large industry conference, proceeded to seriously damage his brand through drunken misbehavior—all in the space of one evening. This might seem like an extreme example, but the truth is that your personal brand is only as strong as your behavior, and every moment counts. Surely it's best to avoid brand damage before it happens (an ounce of prevention is worth a pound of cure), but as human beings, we all make mistakes from time to time. These mistakes can occur in an instant (one thoughtless post on a social media site), a few hours (as in the case of the drunken board member), or over time. Knowing how to repair the damage to your image, and the trust you have worked so hard to establish, is essential. In this chapter, you'll find a few strategies—and stories of inspiration—to help get your personal brand back on track.

> Your personal brand is only as strong as your behavior, and every moment counts.

Name Change

A good friend of mine had some real troubles as a youth. She didn't feel comfortable with who she was and just didn't fit in with the other kids. She was very misunderstood and simply didn't understand why the other kids wouldn't accept her for the wonderful person she was. Her family moved to another city and she came up with a new plan to "manage her brand." She decided she was going to change how others perceived her. She determined what she wanted people to think and know about her that made her such an interesting and unique person and established how she would communicate those items to her new friends. She changed how she dressed, what she communicated, and she even changed her first name. It was an amazing transformation. The new school accepted her and she made a few good friends. She had changed her life by proactively managing her brand.

This example might seem extreme. I believe, however, that we have the ability to change anything we want about ourselves if we are truly committed to certain beliefs and behaviors. It is my observation that people will accept the change if they see frequent enough behaviors to support them. How many times have we heard, "She used to be . . ." or "He didn't used to . . ."? People will typically give someone a break or numerous chances to prove her behavior.

"I Have to Change, or Else I May Lose Them"

Recently I was teaching a group of executives the concepts of personal branding at a conference in Denver. The executives were all feeling pretty good as I went through the concepts of what people thought of them today compared to what they needed people to think. At the height of their moment of feeling really good about their respective brands, I hit them with the tough questions. What is your brand at home? What does your spouse think of you? What do your children think of you?

The looks on the faces in the room told the story. So many of these men and woman had worked relentlessly to build a great brand at work, but had ignored their brand at home.

One gentleman came up to me in tears after the session. He told me he was embarrassed by the reality of what he had created with his personal brand with his family. He realized his brand traits were "too tired to do things," "not present when he was there," "always watching TV," and "family isn't his priority." He shared how much he loved his family, and he felt that they would understand his being tired and wanting to come home and relax. He looked at the years of missed conversations, lost time with his daughters, and how his wife learned to just leave him alone so he could wind down after work.

When I shared how I manage my brand with my kids and my wife, it opened his eyes to what he wanted. He was so far from the desired brand, however, that the task of repairing it seemed almost impossible.

His eyes were red and glassy as he spoke about how his family saw him and how he felt it could never change. His habits and behaviors were so clearly established that he felt he could never get his family to believe anything different.

I agreed to work with him over the next couple of years to change his brand.

We started with him writing down on paper his current brand. Many times I will have someone get feedback from others to make sure the brand is clear. In this case, I felt it wasn't necessary because he told me the things his wife and daughters had said to him in the past. It was pretty clear to both of us what they thought of him.

This information was hard to see in writing. He became emotional once again when he looked at the words on the page.

The next step was for him to write down the elements of his desired brand. He wrote down things like "always be present when with my family," "only watch TV with my family," "be involved in activities with my wife," "no drinking when I get home," and "electronic devices never come out around family." I asked him if he felt he could change his behaviors to meet these new desired brand items. He responded, "I have to change, or else I think I may lose them."

We established some steps to help him make these behavioral changes. He would read his desired brand page every day for the first ninety days. We built a list of things he would stop doing and a list of things he could do to improve his focus. He did things like hold hands with his wife when they were together to help be more present with her. He would make eye contact with his girls when he spent time with them. And he was not allowed to bring out his cell phone when in their presence unless it was to do something pertaining to them.

We developed social media strategies to highlight his focus on his family. He identified strategies to emphasize things he loves about his wife and daughters in well-timed social media posts. These were not contrived and untrue. They were true and actually feelings he had about them. He was simply managing his brand to make sure he was perceived for what he really wanted to be versus what he had lazily become.

Over the next two years, I have held him accountable through regular check-ins and discussions. We talk about his brand on a monthly basis. After about three months of working on his brand at home, his wife asked him what had triggered his change in behavior. He shared with her the work he was doing. She confirmed his perception of his old brand and was very excited about his new one.

He has done an excellent job over the two-year period. He hasn't been perfect, but he has stuck to his plan and it is now habit. He is much happier than he was before and has found new energy in his life because of his new brand with his family.

The greatest reward for me was when I met his wife. This time she had tears in her eyes. She spoke with great sincerity when she said, "You changed our family, our home, and our marriage. Thank you so much for what you did for my husband."

My work was simple and easy. I helped him realize he had a brand at home and it probably would have consequences that he didn't want. He had to do the work. It was exciting for all of us to see how a brand could flip-flop in a relatively short amount of time. In just a few short months, his brand started to change, and his new brand completely overtook the old one within a couple of years.

Change *is* possible. If your personal brand needs work, don't put it off. You have the power to change it—by modifying your behavior and communicating to the people you care about most the person you truly are.

> If your personal brand needs work, don't put it off.

Children in Africa Use Branding to Influence Community

Milton Opoya is from a rural community in Uganda. He grew up in poverty, but his parents sacrificed everything, including their house, to ensure he went to school. Selling their house left the family homeless, and they were forced to live under a tree. He ended up attending university and eventually graduated. Through all of this, Milton never forgot the sacrifice of his parents.

Kampala is a community in Uganda that has areas of extreme poverty. As with any region with this level of poverty, there are not only economic issues but also social issues. One of the major problems facing this area is street kids. Unfortunately, many young boys end up living on the street due to cases of abuse and their parents' death. Some families do not have enough room or resources to care for the entire family. Girls are seen as income generators due to dowries, and boys are seen as revenue drains. These children are forgotten because no one wants them. In order to survive, they turn to stealing and other deviant behaviors. Many times, they turn to drugs simply to curb the feeling of hunger. There is no future for them.

In 2007, Milton was working as a bookkeeper for a nonprofit organization. He quickly realized that his true passion was to engage the forgotten children and do something bigger than accounting functions. In 2008, Milton and his wife rented a home and went out to the slums of Kampala to start connecting with the homeless children. He soon found five boys who expressed their desire for a better life. African Child in Need (ACN) was started, and currently cares for twenty-three boys. The organization provides clothing, shelter, basic health care, and education for the boys. Milton is doing this because of the sacrifice his parents made for him, and he is trying to give a voice to the voiceless and hope to the hopeless children of Uganda.

Along with the obvious struggles that these children face, there is another situation that arose. Because of their past as street kids, these children have horrible reputations as thieves and misfits. The neighbors around Milton's home do not want these children in the area, and they do not hide their anger. They verbally assault the children as they come and go, and there are high levels of tension. The boys are seen as very dangerous.

Enter Michael Loeters, one of our clients. For the past few years, Michael has traveled to Africa during his summer holiday in order to give to those in need. He became aware of Milton and ACN, and began working with them. Michael has gone through several branding exercises and conversations with us. He fully understands the importance of personal branding, and he saw a huge opportunity to bring this concept to Kampala.

On his last trip, Michael decided to take some of our concepts and ran two separate personal branding workshops with ACN. The first was with the boys to help them manage their brand, and the second was with Milton. He discussed the concepts:

- You have a brand.

- What is a brand?

- What are you doing to reinforce your current brand?

- Identify your future brand.

- You have the power to change your brand over time.

The boys in the home ranged from eight to eighteen years old. Even with their strained background, they were still typical young boys: They tried to act macho around their friends. They were very into the urban/hip-hop culture, which influenced their speech, dress, dance, and attitude. Sometimes, they lashed out at neighbors in retaliation to verbal abuse, and they were typically treated extremely poorly at school. Teachers frequently called them thieves and told them that they were worthless. They were all good boys, but their image was sadly reinforcing the negative stereotype that their neighbors, teachers, and others had put on them.

During his workshop in Kampala, Michael tried to help them understand how their actions, words, and dress, affect what people think of them. At first, his words didn't have the planned effect. The kids were just blowing it off as another message of growing up or not acting like they felt they needed to act to be cool. Michael then began discussing what they liked and who they listened to on the radio. Unanimously, they answered Lil Wayne, an American rap artist. Michael then asked the boys what they thought of Lil Wayne as a person, not an artist. Again they unanimously answered, "He's a criminal." (We are not representing that this is true about Lil Wayne. It is simply what the kids said.) They said this because of his lyrics, his dress, and the things they heard about him. *Ding!* The lightbulb went off. They quickly understood that their emulating him and others was how people thought of them. Their reputation was being communicated loud and clear, and they weren't happy with the message they were sending.

The second workshop was a one-on-one with Milton. Michael went over the issues that he had discussed with the boys and the importance of Milton's role in reinforcing these concepts to manage their reputations. He is the brand manager. Next, Michael turned his focus to Milton. As Milton has said, ACN gives a voice to the voiceless and hope to the hopeless. This is very true and positive; however, they needed to work on a more powerful message. Milton regularly has to meet with the boys' teachers, the neighbors, other street boys, and community members. It is often hard for him to communicate the importance of his organization's work. Michael and Milton worked hard and got to the root of what ACN truly does. They are developing the future leaders of Uganda. These boys are taken in and given a chance to develop into family figureheads, community leaders, and leaders of the country. That is a powerful message and shows the potential impact of ACN on the country as a whole.

Michael and Milton worked through a plan to continue to manage the boys' brand, how that tied to ACN, and how ACN could help enhance that reputation.

Now that they are managing their brand, many of the boys are having a different impact on the community. They see themselves from an external perspective versus an internal view. It will take time for the community to completely change its view of these boys. But progress has already been made, and more progress seems likely in the future. ACN is no longer managing the brand of the center or the boys by chance. It is a proactive brand management strategy, and it is working. ACN's brand was on the mend, and the community began to notice the change.

A recent success has shown the boys how powerful personal brand management can be. One of the fifteen-year-old boys has real creative talent. He makes jewelry from beads, and loves the fashion scene. By changing his personal brand, he was able to get acceptance in the fashion community in Kampala, eventually getting models to wear his jewelry during shows. He has started an online store to sell his jewelry, and is gaining recognition for his creative talents. He has gone from being a street kid to a recognized and respected designer in the Ugandan fashion community. He was only able to get this opportunity by changing his brand. The door was opened when others were willing to accept his new image.

After returning from Uganda, Michael posted a picture of him running the branding workshop with the boys. Unsolicited, Milton wrote, "This workshop changed my life!"

Milton is still reinforcing these concepts with his boys, and he is helping them manage their brand. He plans on using this with his new center that he is opening for troubled girls.

CHAPTER 7

No Brand Is an Island

Your Personal Brand at Work (and at Home)

If I lost control of the business, I'd lose myself—or at least the ability to be myself. Owning myself is a way to be myself.

—Oprah Winfrey

Me Inc. Fits in We Inc.

Patrick's father, Roger Sitkins, has been one of the thought leaders in the insurance and risk management industry for over thirty years. He is the most well-known teacher, adviser, and trainer to large insurance agencies in North America. I went to one of his classes in 2003. He taught us that as insurance agents, we were in business for ourselves. Being in business for yourself was expressed in the concept of Me Inc. He quickly expressed that Me Inc. is always part of We Inc. in the insurance agency world.

Technology was not anywhere near as prominent in 2003 as it is today. New technology has advanced, and Me Inc., is now becoming a clearer part of the company brand. The brand of a company is influenced heavily by the individuals within. A quick tweet, post, or Internet comment can boost or destroy a company. When a decision maker can look on the Internet to learn about the staff members who are going to be servicing his account, individual brands start to matter. As I mentioned earlier, I believe every business will soon be required to proactively manage the individual brands of its employees. People are researching the individuals of a company before they do business with them.

Individual brands will come together to become the corporate brand. A corporate brand manager will need to integrate individual brand management into the overall strategy. The individual brands will be the ultimate credibility of the company and may be the primary reason someone chooses to do business with a company. Conversely, employees who embrace a company's values as a part of their personal brand will likely succeed in that company. The combination of the individual brands will become the We Inc. brand.

Recently in a three-day period, I met with a representative of a very large company, and had a meeting with a very successful innovator. Both meetings began with, "Larry, I have done extensive research on you. I have watched videos, read your blogs, and studied what you and your company do." Both of these individuals had researched the company after they had researched my personal information. It was exciting to hear both of them tell me they had researched the industry and determined that they had already decided they wanted to work with me and utilize my companies to partner on new products.

Can you see the power of what I just described? We live in a world where people make decisions on doing business with you before they ever meet you. They make final decisions prior to doing business with you. Your brand as an individual and as a company will combine to create credibility. If these brands align, you've given yourself, and your company, a powerful edge against the competition.

> We live in a world where people make decisions on doing business with you before they ever meet you.

In the past, brand management was all about the company. You worked for Mammoth Corporation, and that fact bestowed upon you a certain measure of respect and stature. That brand "meant something." Less meaningful was your brand as an individual. Sure, personal credibility always mattered. But for the most part, individual employees were expected to uphold the company's brand, rather than establish or manage their own. Call it trickle-down branding, if you like. The organization's brand was pervasive, and it was established from the top.

In contrast, we're moving toward more of a hybrid model of corporate branding, where a company's brand is made up of both a corporate brand and the many individual brands within it. This new model presents challenges at every level. Blending a corporate brand with individual brands can create a powerful combination—but it will also require a great deal of thoughtful strategy and leadership. The pitfalls are many; as individuals manage their own brands, they often misstep. One careless post on social media or poor online profile could seriously harm the greater whole. Being seen on a negative video that goes viral could be the end of a company. The individual and corporate branding of We Inc., and Me Inc., will be part of the strategic objectives of many companies, large and small, as we move forward. The objective will be not only to avoid disasters, but to harness the enormous potential of thoughtful brands working in concert to achieve excellence, however it is defined.

Your Personal Brand Is the Corporate Brand and Vice Versa

There's No Distinction Between Personal and Corporate Brand

Earlier I mentioned the interview Patrick had with Michael Fertik. Michael had great insight when Patrick asked him about the difference between corporate reputation management and personal branding. Michael said, "There is no meaningful distinction between a corporate and personal brand." Unless you are sitting in the bowels of a huge corporation, your personal brand is the corporate brand, and vice versa. The idea that these two brands are connected should scare many executives. There is little focus in the insurance industry right now on organizations helping their employees manage their personal brand. Well, as you can see, there is a big risk here. One employee could cause a lasting effect on your organization. I would even argue that the person in the bowels of a corporation could also create great damage. Most of the world had never heard of Jerry Sandusky prior to the Penn State events of the past few years. He wasn't even an employee when he was committing many of these crimes. Personal brand damage will be on the front pages of the news on a daily basis, because it is exciting and easily accessible.

It Doesn't Have to Consume Your Life

One of the biggest pushback comments that we typically get when discussing personal branding is the amount of time (perception) that this takes. The reality is that this doesn't have to consume your life. Michael told Patrick, "You don't have to be a social media power user. You just need to be in the stream (whatever that looks like for you), doing your thing."

The Cost of Doing Nothing

Michael also said, "If you don't have potential clients coming to you on a regular basis; if recruiters aren't approaching you weekly; if opportunities aren't knocking down your door, then you are doing something wrong."

What does that mean to you? What does that equate to in lost revenue? The cost of not proactively managing your brand could be millions of dollars. That is not an exaggeration.

At the conclusion of the conversation, Patrick said he "felt energized because though it is a scary time in history and many individuals and organizations are falling victim to brand damage, the good news is that there are several resources and easy-to-use tools to help you manage your brand and reputation."

Your In-House Brand

I was recently working with a group of salespeople on a project to increase their sales results. We worked through many concepts, but personal branding really hit home with one of the participants. In the middle of my teaching, he blurted out, "I know why I am struggling! I manage what people think of me outside of this office every day. I focus on getting the world of clients and prospects to think certain things about me. My problem is that I do *nothing* to manage what people think of me inside the office."

He was correct. He was in such a hurry to manage what clients and prospects thought of him, he didn't realize how important and valuable it was for his in-house colleagues to know him in that same way. He had time management problems and external brand problems, because the people on his internal teams didn't like him and frequently spoke negatively about him in public. His assistant would roll her eyes and give negative comments about him to clients. His brand was negative because he didn't realize he had to manage his brand internally.

He has taken a 180-degree turn since this discussion. He was able to get clarity around his desired internal brand. He changed behaviors and spent more time working on the items that needed to change. He spent more time and energy with his team to help them get to know him better and understand his values and his deeper self. He also spent more time getting to know them as people (part of the brand he wanted to have). He knows it is going to take a long time to change this internal brand. He also realizes that if he doesn't make these changes, he will never reach his potential.

An internal brand will determine your workload, what you receive in communication, your chances for promotion, your potential trust, the response to your requests, and a lot more. What do people think of you inside of your organization? If you are a "get it done" person, more work will come your way. If you are a person who makes it hard for people to give you information, you won't get much information. I worked for a manager early in my career, and every time I gave him a report he would turn around and give me numerous projects based on that report. His brand was "when he gets information he causes more work for others." So I stopped giving him reports. He would get frustrated when he couldn't get the information, but his frustrations were easier to deal with than the huge workload he in turn piled on me. This manager probably wishes he could get more information, but he won't, as long as his brand reflects the notion that he causes more work.

> What do people think of you inside of your organization?

If you don't get things done, others may not get things done for you. If you don't get things done, you may not get high-quality projects given to you. That could impact your promote-ability. Your internal brand will determine the success of your job.

Identifying our current brand requires honest feedback from others, good self-analysis, and frequent reviews. These are worthless, however, if we don't clarify what we want people to think of us.

I found this to be so powerful for me this past year that I wrote keywords on a piece of paper and posted it on my office wall. These four words (intelligent, servant, thought leader, and disciplined) were what I wanted people to think of me as the leader of my companies. I believe people think these four things of me now, because I looked at them and was constantly reminded to be that person.

As you develop your brand, be sure to recognize that you have both an internal and external brand. Manage both, and you will increase productivity and overall success.

Internal Versus External

One of my longtime clients asked me to work on some growth strategies in his business. We looked at a lot of areas and found that his corporate and personal branding needed a lot of work. We spent time developing strategies and tactics to improve his and the company's brand.

When we finished, he dropped his head and said, "I don't have time to do all of this. Which of these two—corporate or personal branding—is more important? I will do that one first, and if I get the time, I will do the other one."

My response was not what he wanted to hear. I could not give a reason for either one to be more valuable or important than the other. An individual could damage his company and put him out of business in a day. His company brand was critical to delivering the right message to the market about what his company was and what it did.

My advice was to find something else that was less important and make sure these two items were moved to the top of the list. He wasn't happy with his current results, so I asked him what the cost of doing nothing would be. He understood and acted.

The results have been excellent. The company has increased its sales, and the individual salespeople are thriving. They have resurrected the sales of many of their staff just through the creation of strong personal branding.

When I started my first management job in 1988, I had a vice president tell me, "You can't solve all your problems with revenue . . . but you can sure cover up a bunch of them." Corporate and personal branding is a step toward more revenue. It won't solve all the problems, but it will give you a chance to cover up a bunch!

It is a choice. We have a lot of risks we have to manage in our businesses. Branding is one of those risks. Insurance is even now being sold to assist with brand damage (reputation risk management); it has become that prominent. We must choose which risks to spend time on. I contend that branding may be one of our most critical risks to manage.

Polishing the Family Brand

As I mentioned in Chapter 1, my family and I often discuss our personal brands. I sit down with each of my five daughters on a regular basis to check in about our goals, our progress, and any stumbling blocks we've encountered. This might sound like a series of mandatory sessions involving handwringing and mea culpas, but in fact it's great fun for all of us. We've come to look forward to these conversations. As with all aspects of personal branding, it comes down to being understood—being seen, heard, and valued for who you really are. What could be more enriching to discuss as a family?

This isn't a book about family dynamics, and I'm not a licensed counselor. But I thought it would be useful to share a few conversation-starters that parents can try with their children, in order to get a dialogue going.

Keep in mind that as challenging as defining and maintaining a personal brand can be for us adults, it can be even more challenging for young people. They are often facing pressures in every area of life—family, friends, academics, and sports. The question "Who are you?" can be daunting to attempt to answer head-on.

Being a young person, particularly an adolescent or teen, has always been a confusing time of life. That's nothing new. What is new, however, is that we live in an amplified world—a world that none of us could have imagined just a decade or two ago. Social media is even more of an echo chamber for young people than it is for adults. Social pressure, acceptance, popularity, standards of beauty and body image, questions of identity—these are all coins of the realm online. If, like me, you're in your fifties (or older), try to imagine what sixth grade would have been like with Facebook in your life. "Friends," "likes," "shares," photos from parties you might or might not have been invited to, grades, college acceptance news . . . not a pretty picture, is it?

Personal brand management shouldn't feel like homework or "tough love." It's about identifying the best parts of yourself and sharing them with others. There's no magic bullet, of course, but this clarity and self-awareness can help minimize the confusion and pain most kids go through during the rough patches of adolescence.

When discussing personal branding with young people, keep the following realities in mind:

- **The Internet amplifies everything.** Missteps can be costly, and it isn't easy to undo the damage once it's done. A careless joke, a harsh judgment, a lapse in judgment—these can stay with us a long time.

- **Context matters.** A comment you might make to a close friend may not be appropriate to make in front of a large group, where your best interests may not be protected.

- **Consistency is everything.** When we're being pulled in many directions, facing expectations from family, friends, teachers, teammates, and more, it's helpful—and important—to connect with our core values and principles. These can guide us to do the right thing.

- **Internal and external brands exist in a family context, too.** Just as we have an internal or "in-house" brand at work, seen by colleagues, staff members, and others on our own team, as well as an external one, seen by clients and others in our industry, so, too, we have internal and external family brands. How do outsiders view your family? And most important, how do your loved ones regard you—as a caring parent, a tireless advocate, someone who is always there? Or in some other way?

Family Brand Discussion Questions

What words describe our family's core values?
What makes us special and unique, as a family?
When are you most proud to be a member of our family? Why?

If our family could have just one bumper sticker displayed on our car, what would it say?

If our family was a sports team, which one would it be? Who would each "player" be?

How could our family "team" be even more successful? In what areas do I need more practice?

Personal Brand Discussion Questions

What are the moments that bring you the most joy?

When are you most proud of yourself?

If you had an extra Saturday or Sunday next weekend, how would you choose to spend it?

What's your favorite place on Earth? What do you most like to do there?

What would you do if the only opinion that mattered was your own? What would a typical day in that universe look like for you?

How would you spend your free time if you never had homework?

What would your best friend say is your best quality? What would you say his or hers is?

What are three things you wish people knew about you?

CHAPTER 8

Profiles in Personal Branding (for Better or Worse)

Character is much easier kept than recovered.
—Thomas Paine

Buzz Lightyear: One Brand Can Make a Difference

Nick Bair was one of the most positive people ever to walk this earth. At the age of sixteen, he was diagnosed with cancer. He ended up beating it twice and finally lost the battle the third time. He was nineteen years old when he passed away.

Patrick and I came to know of Nick and learn his absolutely inspirational story shortly before he passed. During the three and a half years that Nick went through treatments, got better and then much worse, he always remained positive. As a two-time cancer survivor and knowing the importance of cancer research in children, Nick started a nonprofit called Wacky Warriors. The concept is for people doing races, such as bike races, marathons, triathlons, and 5K fun runs, to dress up wackily and raise money for survivors and research. Nick wanted to do something for others who were in the same situation as him. He wanted to make a difference by helping young people manage the challenges of cancer. Thousands of people have had the desire to help, just like Nick. Unfortunately, it can be difficult to get the message out and make a difference. A lot of charities and programs compete for donors and supporters of these types of programs. Nick, however, found a way to create a strong brand that made a big difference and continues to make a difference after he has left us.

While in treatment, Nick dressed up at the hospital to keep things light. He wore wear funny wigs, and he even dressed as Buzz Lightyear for a marathon. He was too sick at that point to run the full race, so he sprinted and beat everyone the first ten meters, and then he pulled off of the course. (A video of Nick in his Buzz Lightyear outfit is on the Wacky Warriors website at wackywarriors.org.)

Nick created a brand of being fun, having a positive focus, and having gratitude for everything in life. This brand and his dedication to that brand generated a tremendous following for his charity.

Patrick and I learned about Wacky Warriors and what Nick and his family were doing, and it truly inspired us. Nick had a "never quit, total positivity, make the most out of life, and inspire others" mentality. There are thousands of nonprofits out there, but Nick and his brand were extremely positive and powerful, and that made us want to get involved. His passions are exuded in the Wacky Warriors guidelines:

1. Pay it forward through service to others.

2. Always have something exciting to look forward to.

3. Have fun!

I was so motivated by Nick and Wacky's cause that I decided to race for Wacky Warriors. I trained diligently for months to get ready for the Leadville 100, which is the toughest mountain bike race in the United States. I set a goal and began raising money and awareness for Wacky Warriors. Three weeks prior to the race, I suffered a bad training accident. I hit a rock with my pedal, which sent me over the handlebars and straight down onto the trail. This left me with a separated shoulder, torn ligaments, and broken bones in my arm and hand. Patrick called to check on me that day, and we spoke as I was leaving the hospital. He asked if my injuries were going to put me out of the race. My reply was, "Oh hell no. I've come too far, and I'm doing this for Nick."

Within two days I was back on the bike preparing and training for Leadville. I ended up not only competing in the race but also completing it. It was insane to do, but I had to do it. Even with all of those injuries, the Wacky Samurai (my wacky costume) fought through the pain, exhaustion, and elements to cross the finish line. I had a picture of Nick pinned on my glove. I knew that nothing would have stopped Nick if he had the opportunity to race, and that kept me going.

With all of that said, I never met Nick. He had planned on making it out to Colorado to see me race, but his fight with cancer ended before the Leadville 100 race.

Nick's brand was so powerful that his determination, positive attitude, gratitude, and drive inspired me, and continues to inspire others to push themselves to their limits while helping a great cause. Nick may not have known just how powerful his message was or how clear his brand was received, but I am certain that it has forever changed the people who knew him and know of his story.

A brand can reach farther than your presence. Prior to the Internet, a brand reached only as far as the physical presence of the individual and his immediate relationships. The Internet has expanded a person's brand to become accessible to anyone who desires to find it. Access to information allows for a brand to reach a long way, very fast. Nick created a brand that influenced others. His brand made a difference, and it still is thriving after his life. Nick was just a normal kid living a normal life. When he realized he had an opportunity to have greater purpose, it was through his brand that he was able to create a bigger personal platform. People continue to dress in wacky clothes for races all over the country.

Strategic Coach

Strategic Coach is a business/entrepreneur coaching organization located in Canada. It is an intellectual capital machine that creates more useful tools than you could ever use in your lifetime. Dan Sullivan is the founder of the organization, and he is the brand. Early on, people would go to Strategic Coach classes to learn from Dan. As the programs became more popular, he hit a plateau. The demand for classes quickly became greater than his time would allow. He has done a great job of bringing other highly talented facilitators in, but he is still the brand. In order to get Dan, you have to pay a premium. He as the *part* is still greater than the *whole* that is the organization.

Even though Dan is still the premium brand, the individual facilitators have done a great job of developing their respective brands in the marketplace. Now participants not only choose to attend a Strategic Coach class because of the facilitators, but they also choose to attend or not attend a class based on the facilitators. They have a sense of who the individuals are and what value they will receive by attending certain groups. The facilitators of Strategic Coach have brands that have allowed Dan Sullivan to maximize his brand, but now the individual brands create a bigger company brand. This serves as a great example of how individuals can heavily influence a company's brand for the better.

Energy Drinks

The whole is not unlike every other drink. Companies like Monster Energy and Red Bull use packaging and product placement to appeal to its target audiences, but what they have done better than most is their endorsement strategy. These companies understand that the market trusts the public figures that they idolize, so these energy giants make sure that these high-profile people choose them over their competitors. For example, Monster has looked at its target demographic and connected with athletes who appeal to that group. They sponsor athletes in two-wheel dirt sports, two-wheel asphalt sports, action sports, snow sports, watersports, and more. There are honestly too many athletes to count on their site. They also sponsor musicians, celebrities, and even the Monster girls. This strategy of promoting "the parts" has certainly led to the great success of "the whole."

Then there's Red Bull. Its Stratos project recently was an endorsement for Felix Baumgartner to skydive—from space! Is Red Bull trying to colonize Mars? Is it interested in space exploration? No. Its product is an energy drink. So why would the company invest so much in a guy jumping out of a balloon? (The total amount was undisclosed, but it is clear that a sizable investment was put up.) Simple: its brand! It sells more than energy drinks; it sells an image and a lifestyle. Not only did Felix's stunt enhance this lifestyle, but Red Bull wanted to add to his daredevil brand as well.

These Are the Things That Don't Belong

Patrick is an active observer of celebrity brands. It helps him see an amplified version of what can happen to a brand at any level. Here are some examples of what he has seen with eccentric brands:

> A symbol, Slim Shady, *Born Villain*, a few knights, disco stick, Young Money . . .

Not all brand items have to conform or even be fully understood. They do, however, have to be powerful. Prince, Eminem, Marilyn Manson, Kiss, Lady Gaga, and Nicki Minaj are prime examples of this. These entertainers found a way to break out of the traditional mold and brand themselves as something very unusual. They strive to do things that are considered different and strange, and they always make people question them. Whether you enjoy their music or not, one thing can't be disputed—they have found ways to completely differentiate themselves in a very crowded market. Their antics, dress, words, and presence have defied what is normal. Much of their success has undoubtedly come from their branding efforts.

Other examples of powerful personal brands in the entertainment world are Jimmy Buffett and Kenny Chesney. Both of these legends were at one point in their careers country singers. They both had mild success as traditional country acts. Their mega success didn't come until they found a creative brand that spoke to a very niche group. First Buffett and then Chesney carved out their sound, stage, and persona around the island life. They sing about boats, beaches, and bars, and they have ballads about the good life on the sand. They have created a cult following by managing a reputation that their target audience loves.

Pursue Your Passions

Mark Rollins is an insurance agent by profession, but he will tell you that he is much more than that. There is a group of very innovative agents out there, but they are unfortunately lumped in with the rest. When someone says "insurance," the response is usually immediate, powerful, and *negative*. It is extremely hard for insurance agents to brand themselves as progressive and different. For a long time, Mark was in that group of innovative agents who had a hard time convincing the marketplace that he was truly different from his competition. After years of trying, our longtime friend and client finally found the winning combination. He went with his passion and focused on his brand.

Mark is driven to help those in need. He was actually the one who got Patrick and countless others involved with Bridges to Community. He donates a lot of time and resources to local and global charities. He does this because he truly cares. It isn't self-serving. He finally found a way to combine his career with his passion, and NonProfit Guard was created.

Mark created a personal brand and program that focuses on helping nonprofit organizations. By differentiating himself through creative naming, packaging, content creation, and proactive management of his brand, he is now known as the nonprofit expert. He has created processes, blogs, video resources, social media, connectivity portals, and tools specifically for this niche. He is the go-to guy for risk management advice in the nonprofit world.

Fighting Dolphins

I played football; Patrick's sport was baseball. During his freshman year at Jacksonville University, the season schedule was packed full of games against elite, top-tier baseball programs. During one of his team's many encounters with Florida State University, he learned an important lesson in the power of branding and reputation.

The team traveled to Tallahassee to take on the Seminoles around midseason. Both teams were ranked in the Top 25 in the NCAA at the time. They were having a great year, and the Seminoles were, too (they are consistently ranked in the Top 25). FSU beat Jacksonville a majority of the games during his time at JU.

Patrick was hanging out in the outfield of Mike Martin Field with several other pitchers and position players during pregame batting practice. They were shagging balls, joking around to keep things light, and also talking about the game. One of the catchers said something that stuck with him. He said, "I was talking to some of their guys over the summer, and we were talking about both programs. They told me that there is not a huge difference between the talent in most of the Division I schools. Most programs have great players, but the difference is in attitude and prestige. There is a certain arrogance that comes with playing for a top-tier program. They know there is an intimidation factor at play every time they step on the field."

They were right. I am sure it was intimidating playing against schools that they grew up watching. They were also right about talent. Professional athletes come from a wide variety of schools, and plenty of them didn't even play Division I. There is certainly a well-earned respect that those top-tier players from the top Division I schools received and continue to get even after their playing days.

Talk about the power of reputation.

Motor City Bad Boy

Dennis Rodman was part of the 1988–1990 championship Detroit Pistons teams. Back then, he was an extremely talented basketball player who didn't cause a lot of commotion. As his career developed, so did his brand. He went from another talented guy who blended in to the rock star that he is still known as today. He began dyeing his hair crazy colors, wearing makeup, and at times dressing like a woman. He had an outrageous off-court reputation.

Similar to Brian Bosworth, Terrell Owens, and Chad "Ochocinco" Johnson (Seahawks, 49ers, and Bengals, respectively), Dennis Rodman had a pretty negative reputation. He and the others were not people you would want your kids to emulate or aspire to be. But they all have done something powerful: they created a clear, differentiated brand. While I don't condone much of what these guys are known for, you have to give them credit. They have found ways to create a lasting impression on the marketplace. There is some merit in that.

More than twenty years later, Dennis Rodman is still in the news. He is involved with North Korean politics, and continues to create news and media. In July 2013, he suggested he should receive a Nobel Peace Prize for his relationship and intervention in North Korea. Rodman has continued to display outrageous and unexpected behaviors, and remains a front-page news celebrity.

The Bank

Patrick told me a powerful branding story of how a company image was heavily impacted by the individual brands in the organization. Patrick said he walked into his bank on a Friday afternoon around

2:00 p.m. Two personal bankers were up front, a manager was roaming around the lobby, and three people stood behind the counter. One of the personal bankers flagged him over as soon as he walked in the door. He sat down and told her that he would like to close one of his accounts. She simply took his card and driver's license and began to process it. There was no discussion about why he wanted to close the account or if there was anything she could do to help.

As he sat silent for a few minutes, he tried to strike up a conversation. "So how are you today?"

"Well, it's Friday, so that's good," she replied without even looking away from her screen. After she finished processing the request, she stood up and told him to follow her to the counter to finalize everything. She walked with him about 85 percent of the way there and then turned around without saying a word. He wondered if he had done something to insult her, or maybe she was just having a bad day.

Next, he was greeted by another woman, who gave him a half smile and said in a monotone voice, "How can I help you?" He told her that he was closing his account and wanted to move some funds around. She got out a slip and began filling it out. While he was waiting, a man went to the window next to him. He seemed to be a regular, since he knew the woman helping him and the man next to her. First, the man asked the woman assisting Patrick how she was. She said, "Oh, I'm okay, I guess. I'd be a lot better if I wasn't working."

Next, the man asked the other bank employee how he was. The employee responded, "It's Friday. I'll be a lot better in four hours."

Patrick couldn't believe what he was hearing. How could this very well-known bank not have employees who were trained on attitude, communication, and client experience?

After everything was finalized, Patrick walked toward the front door to leave. As he made his way out, he took one last glance around the lobby. Every employee, including the manager, had their heads hanging, slouching postures, and almost-expressionless faces, and it was extremely quiet.

This experience was a direct reflection on the bank's brand. It seemed almost exactly in alignment with the negative outlook typically placed on corporate America. Everyone was conforming, robotic in their responses, displaying no passion for their jobs, and certainly receiving no support from the corporate headquarters. Patrick said he felt sorry for these employees, and it made him sad for the bank. His interaction with the employees and the bank's reputation both had a damaging effect on the bank's brand that day. I wonder if a portion of their enormous advertising budget ($1.9 billion in 2011) would have been better allocated toward personal brand training. Based on Patrick's experience, I would have to say yes.

$500 Fine and Loss of Client for Littering

Another story Patrick told about personal brand damage is from a drive home from work one day. He was traveling home from work in semi-rush-hour traffic. As he approached a soon-to-be red light, a work truck cut him off, causing him to jam on his brakes pretty hard. As he sat at the red light, the driver of the truck threw a cigarette butt out of the window. Patrick was already a little upset that the driver had cut him off, but throwing trash (yes, cigarette butts are trash) out of his window onto this beautiful stretch of Florida highway? That was too much. He became furious and wanted to yell at the guy, but Patrick is a relatively peaceful person, plus the light had turned green and the driver had already taken off.

As Patrick and the truck driver came to the next traffic light, Patrick was once again sitting directly behind the same vehicle. As they waited for the light to change, he noticed two interesting things. First, the vehicle had a "How's My Driving?" sticker. That actually made him laugh. The second was the fact that this truck was branded. The logo for his company, a lawn care company, was plastered all over the vehicle. Patrick was actually in the market for lawn service and had originally planned on contacting this company. They were one of the best known in his city, and Patrick had seen their advertisements all over the place. After he had experienced this behavior from this employee, however, there was no way that he would hire that company. He certainly didn't want the driver coming to his house!

It isn't just the leadership or high-profile employees at an organization who need to manage their brands. It is every single employee. Whether they are at the office, in front of a client, on a call, or driving around town, they are sending a message about who they are. This message can be very positive or extremely damaging. The market will take notice of the personal brands of your employees and tie that directly to your company.

Patrick told me after this event that it was too bad there wasn't a cop around during his trip home that day. The driver of the truck could have been stuck with a $500 fine for littering.

CHAPTER 9

Personal Branding for Every Age and Stage

People will forget what you did, people will forget what you said, but people will never forget how you made them feel.

—Maya Angelou

We have worked with numerous types of people to help them define and strengthen their respective brands. The following pages include ideas and examples of how you can do the same. Of course, good advice is never one-size-fits-all, so even with the age breakdowns we've included, you'll need to consider which ideas are best for you. We hope you'll give them a try.

Teens

High Volume Creates Higher Risk

Today's teenagers are the masters of technology usage. They are naturally talented at making the handheld device a part of their life. They sleep with their phone, type faster on their phone than adults can on a keyboard, carry on multiple conversations at the same time, make photography into communication, and think video is part of daily life.

These skills and behaviors are changing our world, and everyone will need to get on board if they want to be relevant in the future. This group is establishing our new norms.

They are also at the highest risk of a big fall, however. They are at high risk of bullying, slander, mistakes, and potentially lifelong brand damage with every move they make. The mental side of this technology use has to be their guide.

My daughters are all doing a very good job of this (I continue to pray). Each of them thinks about her brand and make it part of her daily language. They have shared the branding concept with their friends, and it has become a common language for them. If teenagers and their friends are all aware of how technology will impact their brand, they will do a better job of protecting that brand. This group can watch out for each other.

If they think of technology as a broadcasting device that is telling everyone what to think of her, she will have a chance of successfully managing her brand. Even if she is on a video with someone, realizing the other person may be recording the conversation can be a great mindset. We never know if the person on the other side of the video may have someone else in the room, listening to what we are saying. This happened recently to a friend of mine. He thought he was in a one-on-one video chat. He didn't realize someone he was talking about was sitting in the room, out of the range of the camera. Big brand damage!

Teenagers need to make technology a resource to promote a powerful brand. It is part of their lives and the most common media used to project what they want people to think.

They also need to keep in mind that we live in a world where their brand will stay with them for a while. Thanks to technology, whatever they do today will stay with them in the future. Every decision they make could have long-lasting effects. Teenagers need to be aware and manage this risk.

College Students

Launching to Life

There are certain things that the traditional university lacks when it comes to developing young professionals. Parents, business owners, and managers are seeing more and more graduates ill-equipped with the necessary tools to handle their transition to the post-scholastic phase. This is extremely concerning.

In Chapter 3, we mentioned Matt Morehead, CEO of Launch2Life, a program that gives young adults financial planning, network building, résumé writing, and interview skills, and even helps them craft their brand. We sat down with Matt to discuss what separated the successful graduates from the not-so-successful ones. He was kind enough to walk us through the information he presents during his professional presence sessions. We began our discussion around the fact that everyone has a brand. We joked and equated it to pregnancy—you can't be *kind of* pregnant. You either are or you aren't. The same goes for your personal brand or, as he describes it, your professional presence. Once he drives that point home, he then helps them examine what people think of them by walking them through a series of questions. He asks them if they are seen as:

- Someone who is polished and "put together" or someone who's a mess
- Someone who consistently maintains a high level of energy or someone who has major mood and energy swings

- Someone who is confident or someone who lacks confidence

- Someone who is grateful and appreciative or someone who has an entitlement mentality

- Someone who is fun and interesting to be around or someone who is boring and brings very little to each interaction

- Someone who is always on time and ready to go or someone who consistently shows up late and underprepared

- Someone who is organized or someone who is disorganized

- Someone who takes care of his/her health, nutrition, and appearance, or someone who is out of shape and sloppy with his/her appearance

- Someone who talks first and listens second or someone who listens first and talks second

- Someone who drinks and socializes responsibly or someone who loses control

- Someone who spends his or her money frivolously or someone who is careful with his or her money

Notice the above questions are about character traits, not skills. Skills can certainly be a part of your brand, but your personal brand goes much deeper than that. Skills and knowledge are assumed. They are what got you into the school of your choice or your job. Your true brand is more than skills and intellect; it is your reputation. If you are having a hard time defining your brand, seek out those who have seen and interacted with you frequently over a significant period of time (a year or more) and are not family members. I did this very early in my career. Looking at myself and trying to think about my brand and reputation was very difficult. I asked Dianne, one of my best friends from high school; an old coach; a coworker; and my dad what they believed my unique abilities to be. It was extremely beneficial to get their input. It was great to see that my thoughts and what they saw were in alignment. I also saw items that I had never really considered to be who I am. I took a few of those and worked hard to incorporate them into my brand. Discovering your current brand begins by having the courage to interrogate your reality.

All of us can craft a personal brand over a short period of time by giving new acquaintances a first impression of who we are. A true personal brand, however, is about who you are, day in and day out. What if you don't like your current brand? Can you change it? Absolutely, but it can take many years. In the personal branding space, being a young person just starting out is actually a huge advantage. Your slate is largely clean except for what a few friends and acquaintances know about you. Most of these people will have little effect on your future. Yes, there are things that can permanently damage your brand, but you can develop the brand you want much more easily early on in life and in your career.

Matt told us that he sometimes gets feedback from young people. "I don't want to live my life worrying about what others think of me. I just want to be myself. If they don't like that, then tough." Personal brand and professional presence aren't about us all conforming. Again, your brand has to differentiate you; it is certainly about being an individual and being yourself.

. You get to choose the elements of your brand. You will always have people in this world who don't like you and will judge you unfairly. That's part of life. Personal brand is about being genuine and consistent. Authentic relationships are built on consistency. I can't build a great relationship with you if I don't know what I am going to get from one interaction to the next.

If I know who you are (through your brand), I can first decide to form a relationship with you or not and then adapt my interactions with you based on your brand. I know what I am getting. Personal brand also tells me about your judgment. From what you post online to what you choose to wear to meetings, I get to assess your judgment. Do I trust your judgment? If I'm your employer, do I trust your judgment enough to allow you to interact with my best clients?

We once had an employee who was loved by many of our clients. This person was outgoing, helpful, and fun at events—a little too fun. We started noticing behavior and getting feedback from clients that was very negative and certainly against the brand we were building at our company. Stories of inappropriate behavior and partying began to circulate among our clients. We approached this employee several times and attempted to help her manage her personal brand more effectively. Unfortunately, she could not effectively manage her professional presence. Because of this, we were not comfortable placing her in front of clients. After a large investment of time and energy, we knew that this employee was not willing to change, and our trust in her had been damaged beyond repair. We eventually had to let her go.

You Have to Earn the Right

Just as we discussed above, we tend to get feedback from young people who say that they want to just be themselves. They don't care what people think about them. They want to be free to express themselves, just like Mark Zuckerberg. Yes, we get that reference a lot.

Let's think about this for a second. Yes, Mark is very open and honest, and he really doesn't care what people think about him. There is a reason. He's earned the right to think that way. We believe that there is a direct link between what you've accomplished in life and what you can get away with. Another way to say this is that your level of self-expression has to be in alignment with your accomplishments.

There is a hierarchy. If you are in a school organization, team, company, or any group, you have seen this phenomenon. The higher up in a social structure, the more you can get away with. The status of a person is directly related to the amount of shenanigans that are tolerated. These shenanigans can be things like relaxed schedule, conformity to the rules, jokes and statements that are allowed, loudly communicating an opinion, interaction with authority, etc. The reason that these people tend to get away with more is simple: they have earned the right.

Early on at Jacksonville University and then later on when Patrick was starting his career, he was extremely reserved. He would only insert his thoughts or opinions when forced. He toned down what he did online, kept his private life extremely quiet, and didn't really let people know who he was. Looking back, it may have been a bit extreme, but his reasoning was that he hadn't earned the right. Patrick had to prove his value to the team and the organization. Senior classmen had proven themselves and could be more animated, opinionated, and visible. Patrick was just one of three freshmen on the team. It was tough to be taken seriously, until baseball season came. He began to form stronger relationships and let his true personality show, but only after making the travel squad and actually getting some playing time. The same went with his career. He was surrounded by high-level executives as partners and clients. It wasn't until he had proven his value that he could start to express himself a little more and let people in. There are certainly things that he does, says, and expresses now that he wouldn't have even dreamed of early on. These things aren't bad; they are just opinions. Patrick feels like he's earned the right to say the things he does and act the way he does. It's not easy to get to that place though.

Right on the Cusp

Those of us who escaped the both awesome and terrifying social networking age in our younger years often wonder what life would have been like if all this technology had been around when we were in college. Would dating have been a lot easier? Could class notes have been shared on a larger scale? Could we have all known what was going on all over campus? Those would have been cool things to have, but what about the damage this could create? Posted pictures of the baseball initiation party, a video of your twenty-first birthday recorded on a smartphone and posted to YouTube, a late-night post on that soccer girl's wall that you forgot about until the next morning, your parents finding out about your speeding ticket or new tattoo via Twitter—oh, the humanity! Fortunately for my peer group, these were not possible. Unfortunately for today's college-age student, it's a reality.

We often jokingly say "Thank god that stuff wasn't around when we were in school." We weren't that wild of a group (not any more than any other college kids). The part that scares us is that we wouldn't have had a clue how to manage all of this. Some of our youthful mistakes could be much more than memories today. With technology and the way information is shared, these could very easily be relived via a variety of media.

With Great Power Comes Great Responsibility

Voltaire was right.

As a college student, you have had access to and will continue to see the creation of powerful technology, media, and tools to help you. Many of these will directly affect your brand. As illustrated above, many of your choices, interactions, and communications can quickly become public information. It is up to you to utilize these tools to positively communicate your reputation.

Brand management is not solely technology driven. It may be easy for a tech-savvy student to "manage the press" by un-tagging pictures and deleting damaging content, but what about your reputation? This goes far beyond technology.

You have probably heard the phrase "It's not what you know, it's who you know." This is an extremely accurate statement. We are not suggesting that just knowing people will help you succeed post-college; however, it certainly helps. You never know who will be able to help you down the line. It could be a professor, a coach, a roommate, a friend's parent, etc. Since anyone could possibly be a great connection later on, it seems logical that you should start now managing what people think of you.

Branding isn't something that you can put off until after graduation. You need to start now. Think about who you are currently and, more important, who you want to be. Ask yourself how you can develop into that. What resources will you need? Who do you know that could help you get there? Who could be a possible mentor? What things support your current and future brand? What could damage your brand slightly? What could have a lasting negative effect?

College is a fantastic time of growth, learning, and development. Don't waste the knowledge, interactions, and social environment. You can learn a lot about what you want and what you need to avoid.

Family

The Family Impacts the Individuals

A family has a brand, just like a person does. I have seen family brands keep kids from being successful, and I have seen family brands create opportunities. A family brand has a huge impact on the opportunities presented to and eliminated from that family.

I have seen coaches not want kids on teams because of the brand of a family. I have seen kids put on teams because of the family brand. This is true for sports, music, dance, church activities, school programs, and more. Your family brand can be a powerful thing to manage.

How do we manage a family brand? Here you go:

1. Sit down as a family, and determine what you want your brand items to be. You will basically answer the question "What do we want people to think of us as a family?" The answers will be things like hardworking, honest, selfless, caring, philanthropic, and so on.

2. Remember that language drives culture. Parents and kids have to consistently use language that supports that brand. In our family, "inclusion of others" is a value and a brand item we desire. So in our home, we frequently talk about inclusion. We challenge our kids when we feel that they are not including others. The frequency of the language will drive the behaviors.

3. Revisit your brand, and talk about how it is being applied in each person's life outside of the home. If each person has to tell one thing she did this week to make our brand a reality, she will be focused on it more often. It will also give you a chance to celebrate when a family member does something in line with your desired brand.

4. Quickly eliminate items that conflict with your brand. If you send a conflicting message to others, it will damage your brand. So in the name of brand management, correct items that contrast. This will actually be easier now, because you will be working on the brand and not attacking the individual.

5. If you revisit every year (make it a New Year's activity), you will keep it fresh and sharp and be able to celebrate what you have accomplished in the past.

Early Career

Managing Perceptions

The early stages of a career are a whirlwind. You have to learn the culture of the organization and how to fit in. There is technical training, business acumen development, organizational skills to develop, contacts to make, meetings to attend—and all of this while trying to prove your value as early as possible. If you are lucky, management will have you in a development program, and they may even have put a plan together with you. We've noticed that personal branding, and management of it, is rarely focused on. Because of this, people early in their careers typically don't see the value in it, or they may think brand management is something for those high up in the organization. Maybe only top producers and key executives need to worry about their personal brand. They may think, all I have to do is work hard and do a good job. Well, first let's look at the reality of your situation.

Your Perception

This organization is lucky to have me. I am going to bring some youthful energy to this stagnant organization. I'll be able to use all this new knowledge. I've got a great opportunity to learn from some of the successful people here. I am going to set the world on fire. I'm going to make a difference. This is awesome!

Your Coworkers' and Managers' Perception

Great, another person to train. He is going to need so much attention up front. I really don't have time for this. This investment better work out. Someone is going to have to show him the ropes. I wonder how long this one will last. Someone needs to break this kid of youthful tendencies.

If You're Related to Anyone in Leadership or Ownership

Amplify doubts about you times ten. Increase hurdles to overcome times ten. Increase the amount of work it will take to effectively manage a positive and powerful brand times ten.

Are You Essential?

The marketplace was much different when I began working with Patrick back in 2006. Back then, there was a free agent–type mentality among employees, especially recent graduates. Companies were investing time, resources, and capital in becoming the employer of choice. Top organizations were focusing almost as much time on recruiting top talent as they were on marketing to potential clients. Around 2008, the market changed dramatically. The free agency market dried up, and suddenly recent grads, as well as seasoned pros, were finding it harder and harder to find and keep a steady job.

We've all heard stories of top executives suddenly without work and applying for entry-level positions, or the college grads who are still living at home because they can't do anything with their degree. Unemployment rates continue to bounce around but remain exceedingly high, especially in the United States, and uncertainty of global economies continues to be a challenge. So what can you do to find a job and keep it if you don't already have one, or maintain or advance your position at your current company? In other words, how can you become essential? Certainly results and excellent performance will help. What about your brand? Do you think it could help you stand out from the crowd? If done correctly, yes, and this will be essential early on in your career. There are several reasons for this.

First, you need to make yourself one of the most valuable assets on the team (or at least be perceived that way) in case of another major market downturn. If you manage a positive and powerful brand internally, people will be more willing to help you and fight to keep you around.

Try reaching out to help others, especially early on. The old saying is true: "They don't care how much you know, until they know how much you care."

You will have a lot of challenges to overcome. Purposefully managing your brand and showing perceived value will help you overcome some of these.

Having a strong brand will set you apart with your clients, vendors, prospects, and centers of influence. Again, results and performance will be key early on. Purposefully managing your brand will help.

We have worked with thousands of individuals in different industries and at different levels of their careers. As mentioned earlier, we used to run a program for salespeople in their early twenties to late thirties. Most of them had been with their respective companies for less than a month, and in some cases the class was their first day on the job. We had one person say, "I don't even know where my desk is."

We became very good at spotting those who had "it" and those who didn't. Those who had "it" could typically look at themselves and identify their natural talents, value, differentiation, and future brand. They could take their brand and truly manage what others (employees, clients, prospects, and centers of influence) thought of them. It was truly a foundation for their success.

Over the four years of running the class, we kept an informal list of those participants who had "it," the ones we knew would be successful. Not all of them stayed in the sector they were in, but all of them are still very successful in their careers.

Professional Presence

This is an extremely important element in your personal presence, especially early on in your career. Professional presence is the way you present yourself verbally, in writing, online, and visually. All four areas have to be managed in order to maintain a strong personal brand inside of your organization and in the marketplace.

Verbal

Managing your professional presence while speaking is more than the words that you are saying. It's about your interaction, tone, posture, and listening skills. Without the proper mix, it won't matter what you have to say. Here are some things to consider:

- Look people in the eye when speaking and listening.

- Like, no youthful words, um, okay? Totally, you know?

- Actively listen and respond appropriately.

- Show a general interest in your audience.

- Be interesting by telling stories.

- Be relentlessly prepared.

- Use tone and posture to enhance your words.

Written

Writing has become a lost art. Sure, you took basic grammar, language, and writing courses at some point in school, but are you prepared to communicate effectively in the professional world? Unfortunately, technology is damaging our ability to correctly communicate. Texting, emailing, and IMing have brought about a new language specific to the technology. These are not appropriate in the business world (most times). Follow these guidelines:

- Be concise, but give all of the information requested or needed.

- LOL! No abbreviations. One of Patrick's CEO clients is not the most tech-savvy individual at times. For months, a new, younger employee of his used the LOL abbreviation a lot in his email communications. One day, this CEO made an offhand comment to someone else in his office about the new employee. He said, "This is a bit inappropriate. In a lot of his emails, he says, 'Lots of love.'" Needless to say, the CEO's coworker got a kick out of this when she explained to him that LOL meant "laugh out loud." Don't assume that everyone knows what you are trying to say with abbreviations, especially in more formal communications.

- Always treat emails like actual letters. Assume that your communication will get passed around.

- Personality is okay, but make sure you keep your tone professional.

Online

We addressed this subject earlier in the book. There are some specific items to include for the early-career group:

- Never complain about your work situation, supervisors, hours, etc.

- A balance of personal and professional information, posts, images, etc., is best.

- Avoid controversial opinions unless you have accurate information, are ready to back them up, and can stand your ground. Examples of controversial topics include politics, religion, and sexual orientation.

- Your profiles very clearly communicate your brand. Proactively manage them.

- Determine what type of profile you have (see "Seven Types of Profiles," page 79).

Visual

This is another way to proactively manage your brand. As mentioned early on, it takes only thirty seconds (eight for women) to form an opinion of you. Others will then spend the rest of the relationship finding examples to support their initial impression. Here are some items to keep in mind:

- How you dress. We teach people to dress half up from their audience. This can be at work, at dinner, for leisure, or at the gym.

- Be sharp, but blend.

- Arrive on time (preferably a few minutes early).

- Take notes when someone is talking to you.

- Create mass and space. Stand up tall, and project confidence.

- Early in your career, you will find a lot of challenges and obstacles to overcome. If you manage your personal brand effectively, then you will have a greater chance at success.

Seasoned Pros

The Learning Cycle

Some years ago, I was introduced to the four stages of competence, which is used in understanding the cycle of learning. The concept was originally developed by Abraham Maslow (though not recognized in his major works), but was later developed at Gordon Training International in the 1970s by Noel Burch. Let me give a quick overview.

In learning, we go through four stages: unconscious incompetence, conscious incompetence, conscious competence, and unconscious competence.

Unconscious incompetence. We don't know what we don't know. This became very evident to me as I listened to my fourteen-year-old daughter talk about how easy it is going to be when she gets to drive. "I am going to be a great driver, Dad! It is so easy."

Conscious incompetence. We know that we are incompetent. The other day, my fifteen-year-old daughter received her learner's permit and got behind the wheel, and she was conscious incompetent. She had no idea what to do, and she and I both knew we were in danger in that moment. This person needs practice to go to the next phase.

Conscious competence. When my daughter drove for a few weeks with her learner's permit, she had to think about every move she made. She is safe and capable. I can see why they don't just give fifteen-year-olds a license to drive. These people don't need practice; they need pressure. As they receive real-world pressure on what they have practiced, they will learn to do things without having to think.

Unconscious competence. This is what many drivers eventually become. I can't say all, because I am amazed daily at drivers' abilities.

When you no longer have to think about what you are doing, however, and you have mastered the skill, you are unconsciously competent. This is the phase we all hope to reach in all areas we choose to learn.

Okay, so what in the world does this have to do with branding? The final phase doesn't end at unconscious competence. The process is actually a circle. The next phase is unconscious incompetence. This is what we see from many seasoned pros. They start looking at themselves as all-knowing experts. They don't need to learn anything new. The ego of these individuals is so large that they would not want anyone to see weakness in their game.

In a world where information is moving faster than at any time in history, the brand of many of these individuals becomes very negative, very fast. These are the people who others roll their eyes at when they think of them. They feel sorry for them because they are stuck in the past.

Seasoned pros' biggest challenge is to stay on top of their game. If you're a seasoned pro, don't get lazy. Don't let your past success keep you from accomplishing a bigger and better future.

Your brand needs to be managed by reading current information, writing blogs about topics and articles, and giving your opinions. You need to be opening new files in the minds of the readers that others haven't thought about in your world of expertise. Look for something new. Look for something to innovate in your area of passion. Make everyone else continue to chase you. Use technology, and embrace the many possible ways of improving your skills.

If you can avoid being branded as "old school" or "out-of-date," you will stand out from the rest and will never have people roll their eyes at you.

End of Career

"Come On, Grandma!"

I had a very good friend tell me he cringes every time his grandma posts anything on social media. He said, "She thinks that she is talking to her friends in the kitchen and doesn't realize her audience."

When I turned forty, I changed my perspective on life. I started to not care what people thought of me as much as I had in the past. I became a little more opinionated and started choosing whom I wanted to please.

When I turned fifty, I changed my perspective on life. I completely didn't care what others thought about me. I was accomplished and successful and just didn't have the time to worry about those who didn't agree with me or didn't like me.

I have heard that when I turn sixty, I will change my perspective again. I will stop caring that others have an opinion about me.

These generalizations are a bit overstated, but they are certainly close to the way my mind works. Our age gives us confidence, and our successes make caring about others' thoughts about us a little less important. Wisdom says, "I can't change what others think of me."

Now for reality. We live in a world where information is readily accessible. We used to be able to retire and move on and live in our small community that agreed with us. This isn't how things work in the modern world. Now we have social media and video capabilities, which are expanding our footprint and our world. So we have to do some things differently if we want to engage with those in our lives. You may not "care" about what I am saying here, but if you do, here are some ideas for great brand management:

1. Realize that social media is bigger than you think. If you wouldn't say something at a country club party where you don't know everyone who is there, don't say it on a social media site. It is not your safe place. You can quickly offend people if you decide to speak as freely there as you do in your kitchen with close friends. You can't control who sees what, and you will miss a lot of feedback (what they say about you when they read it). Keep your comments positive, and look at others' information. Make a game of it. See if you can learn about generations and what is important to them by reading what they post on their sites. My wife and I are "friends" on Facebook with a lot of our kids' friends. We rarely post anything on their comments or status. They kind of forget we are there, but it makes for great intel!

2. Read current events. The better you understand what is going on in the world, the more relevant you will be. Be interesting by knowing what is going on in the world around you.

3. Read something every week that has the opposing view. This will help you understand others. Seek to understand before seeking to be understood. I didn't invent it, but I sure use the idea a lot.

4. Ask a lot of questions, and continue to learn. I don't know this for a fact, but I have heard you can continue to learn (and remember what you learned) into your eighties. Many people stop learning, however, and the brain atrophies. Keep learning, and you will have a brand that others will want to engage.

5. Smile. Too many people who retire stop smiling. Be happy, and let others know you are happy. I know you may be tired, but a warm smile will engage and welcome others.

FINAL NOTE

Patrick and I wrote this because of our success over the last several years, as well as the success of the people we've helped. We are convinced more than ever that personal branding is not only important but also a crucial strategy for anyone. We wanted to share this information with a general readership in order to truly help people. As someone who works daily in this arena for clients (and for myself), I can tell you that personal brand management can get very overwhelming. I encourage you to implement some or most of the strategies that we've shared. Take it one step at a time, and reevaluate often.

At the end of the day, how you approach personal branding is your choice. We sincerely hope that you will take the insights and examples in this book as a call to action. A well-managed personal brand is arguably your best asset in today's competitive and amplified world. With some thoughtful planning and action, you can make the most of the opportunity it presents each one of us.

Good luck!

ACKNOWLEDGMENTS

My first book, *Make the Noise Go Away*, was written due to intense market demand. My clients demanded that I write a book because I couldn't get to all of them. This book was different. I wrote it because I was passionate about it and saw the world shifting.

The shifts in my life, however, made writing it very difficult. My businesses are thriving, my kids are growing up and need me around, and my wife likes having me around. The last few years have been a challenge to find the time to write.

I am truly thankful for my family in every way. They are my inspiration, and they challenge me to be the best I can be. I want to be worthy of being their husband and father. I hope this book helps accomplish that goal, as they have all sacrificed in its writing. Debi, you are my best friend. Tiffany, Wen Jun, Macie, Avree, and Lia, you guys are my lifeblood. Thanks for making me the man I am today. I can't wait to see how you will change me in the future.

I also want to thank my clients and friends who gave me the experiences to write about. Books of interest usually have true stories. Thank you for trying our ideas.

Lee Brower, you have inspired me and helped me be a better me. Much gratitude to you, my friend.

Mike Natalizio, thanks for bouncing ideas around. You are a branding genius.

Patrick, I admire you for your guts and desire to build your own business. Your generation is powerful and will make landmark changes in our world. This book and your input and tireless efforts in bringing examples, intellectual property, and great ideas to personal branding, show just a glimpse of those changes. Thank you and Di for being great friends, and for your endless hours of ideas and writing in this book. We have a lot more to get accomplished. We have to pay for college for your inspiration, Callen and Baby #2!

Roger Sitkins, thank you for providing opportunity.

RESOURCES

Intellectual Innovations
theiionline.com
Assistance in executive brand development and tools and resources to help
business grow.

Quintain Marketing
quintainmarketing.com
Web presence, SEO, web design, technology support and advice, and personal
brand management.

Launch2Life
launch2life.com
Personal development program for twenty- to thirty-year-olds.

Reputation.com
Online reputation management and protection.

Be Influential
be-influential.com
Online portal to create your personal brand. Allows for full portfolio of work,
résumé, videos, and pictures to show others your brand.

AboutMe
aboutme.com
A simple and easy personal brand website design.

PERSONAL BRAND ASSESSMENT

Brand Assessment Guide	Yes	Somewhat	No
Do you define what you want people to think of you?			
Do you have a plan to manage how others think of you?			
Do you know what people think of your current brand?			
Have you eliminated behaviors that could damage your brand?			
Have you built behaviors that positively reflect your brand?			
Is your current brand helping you to reach your goals?			
Do you tell family members your desired brand?			
Do you tell coworkers your desired brand?			

Your Answers:

Yes (3 POINTS): _____

Somewhat (2 POINTS): _____

No (1 POINT): _____

Total: _____

Brand Assessment Guide	Always	Sometimes	Never
Are you involved in social media where your clients, friends, and family are involved?			
Do your key brand items stand out on your social media profiles?			
Do you manage your SEO to be quickly identified on web searches?			
Do you review your brand every six months or less?			
Do you think about or consider your brand every time you post on social media?			
Do you think about your brand when choosing how you dress each day?			
Are you aware of others' brands?			

Your Answers:

Always (3 POINTS): _____

Sometimes (2 POINTS): _____

Never (1 POINT): _____

Total: _____

Combined Total: _____

36–45 = Brand Genius! You get it; your brand is strong. Keep it up.

28–35 = Brand Amateur. Your brand is at risk, but your potential is great if you sharpen some things.

15–27 = Brand Damage. Your brand is potentially in bad shape. You need to get a plan and get to work!

ABOUT THE AUTHORS

Larry Linne is internationally considered a thought leader in business strategy and growth. He has spent more than two decades helping companies and individuals create and manage their brands. Larry is CEO/president/partner of two globally successful companies—Intellectual Innovations and Sitkins International. He is also the author of the Clarion 5 Star top-performing book *Make the Noise Go Away: The Power of an Effective Second in Command*. He sits on the board of directors for HNI Risk Services, NFL Alumni Colorado Chapter, and USA Volleyball Board Selection Committee. He and his wife, Debi, have a foundation called 9.5 Alive that has raised tens of thousands of dollars for orphans worldwide.

Patrick Sitkins is a branding leader and digital marketing and social media expert. He is the founder and CEO of Adaptive Inbound Marketing Solutions, an international strategic branding and digital marketing firm. Connect with him on LinkedIn, Twitter, Google+, or his personal website, patricksitkins.com.